Idaho

WILDLIFE VIEWING GUIDE

Edited by Aimee L. Pope

Adventure Publications, Inc.
Cambridge, MN

Watchable Wildlife Series

EDITOR – Aimee L. Pope, Idaho Department of Fish and Game
CARTOGRAPHY – Stephanie Singer, Bureau of Land Management
ILLUSTRATIONS – © Ward P. Hooper, Hooper Studios, Boise, Idaho
FRONT COVER PHOTO – American avocets by © William H. Mullins, Boise, Idaho
BACK COVER PHOTOS – Bighorn sheep, Mountain goats and Wood duck by © Gary Kramer; Bobcat by © Jim Dutcher
First Edition: 1990, by Leslie Benjamin Carpenter

 ISBN 1-59193-029-4

Published in cooperation with the Idaho Watchable Wildlife Committee

Printed in China

ABOUT WATCHABLE WILDLIFE, INCORPORATED

Watchable Wildlife, Inc. is an independent 501c-3 nonprofit working with communities and state and federal wildlife agencies. Our mission is simple: "To help communities and wildlife prosper."

We accomplish this mission by developing sustainable wildlife viewing programs with our partners. Our areas of focus are our annual conference, publications, and on-the-ground projects.

Our annual Watchable Wildlife Conference is the nation's best vehicle for training and recognizing the works of professionals working in the field of wildlife viewing. Watchable Wildlife, Inc. works hands-on with conservation-minded partners on projects across the continent.

Our Viewing Guide series is a continent-wide effort to meet the needs of North America's growing wildlife viewing public. The guides encourage people to observe wildlife in natural settings, and provide them with information on where to go, when to go, and what to expect when they get there. We believe the presence of wildlife viewing sites near communities will have positive social and economic impacts.

We want wildlife viewing to be fun. However, we also believe it should be an economically viable resource for the host community. In the larger context, we want people to learn about wildlife, care about wildlife, and conserve wildlife.

For more information about Watchable Wildlife, Inc. and our projects, visit www.watchablewildlife.org.

Brown road signs with the binoculars logo let travelers know that they're in a great spot to see some wildlife! These uniform signs are officially approved by the National Department of Transportation and are one example of the programs sponsored by Watchable Wildlife, Inc.

IDAHO WATCHABLE WILDLIFE GUIDE SPONSORS

The Bureau of Land Management administers 12 million acres of public lands in Idaho for the use and enjoyment of present and future generations. The BLM's Watchable Wildlife program promotes responsible wildlife viewing and outdoor ethics. <www.blm.gov>

The U.S. Forest Service administers 21 million acres of public lands in Idaho for "multiple use," including wildlife habitat. These national forests provide a diversity of wildlife habitat supporting birds, mammals, reptiles, amphibians, fish, and plants. <www.fs.fed.us>

The U.S. Fish and Wildlife Service is the principal federal agency responsible for conserving, protecting and enhancing fish, wildlife, and plants and their habitats for the continuing benefit of the American people. <www.fws.gov>

The U.S. Bureau of Reclamation administers land and water providing critical habitat for several wildlife species. These resources offer a vast spectrum of opportunity to observe and study wildlife in its natural habitat. <www.usbr.gov>

The National Park Service conserves and protects resources unimpaired for future generations' public use and enjoyment. In Idaho, NPS administers a national historic park, a national reserve, and two national monuments. <www.nps.gov>

The Idaho Department of Fish and Game administers wildlife management areas, fishing lakes, and fish hatcheries across Idaho. The IDFG is responsible for preserving, protecting, perpetuating, and managing all Idaho wildlife. <www.state.id.us/fishgame>

The Idaho Department of Parks and Recreation administers 26 state parks and state recreation programs "to the end that the health, happiness, recreational opportunities and wholesome enjoyment of the life of the people may be further encouraged." <www.idahoparks.org>

The Idaho Travel Council provides tourism and recreation information to travelers throughout Idaho. The agency publishes an annual Travel Guide and maintains an extensive website of attractions, recreation sites, lodging, and activities. <www.visitid.org>

The Golden Eagle Audubon Society is southwest Idaho's chapter of the National Audubon Society. This organization is dedicated to building an understanding and appreciation of the natural world. <www.goldeneagleaudubon.org>

IDAHO WATCHABLE WILDLIFE COMMITTEE MEMBERS

Special thanks to the past and present members of the Idaho Watchable Wildlife Committee. Your dedication, time, and funds have made this guide a reality.

BUREAU OF LAND MANAGEMENT – Kay Schiepan, Larry Ridenhour, Stephanie Singer, Mark Hilliard, Shelley Davis-Brunner, Allan Thomas

U.S. FOREST SERVICE – Alexis Collins

U.S. FISH AND WILDLIFE SERVICE – Elaine Johnson, Meggan Laxalt Mackey

BUREAU OF RECLAMATION – Steve Dunn

IDAHO DEPARTMENT OF FISH AND GAME – Wayne Melquist, Aimee Pope, Bruce Haak, Jon Beals, Pam Peterson

IDAHO DEPARTMENT OF PARKS AND RECREATION – Larry Mink, Aimee Pope

IDAHO DEPARTMENT OF COMMERCE/IDAHO TRAVEL COUNCIL – Celeste Becia, Carl Wilgus

IDAHO RECREATION AND TOURISM INITIATIVE – Jack Lavin

IDAHO TRANSPORTATION DEPARTMENT – Jeff Stratten

GOLDEN EAGLE AUDUBON SOCIETY – R. L. Rowland

IDAHO WILDLIFE VIEWING GUIDE

IDAHO'S WATCHABLE WILDLIFE by Ward P. Hooper

Idaho artist Ward Hooper painted a masterpiece in honor of Idaho's Watchable Wildlife. The acrylic painting, almost three feet by four feet, depicts various Idaho plant, fish, and wildlife species. The artist attempted to place creatures and plants near the travel regions they might likely exist. If you look closely, the outline of Idaho can be seen. For a poster of this artwork, please see page 5.

IDAHO'S WATCHABLE WILDLIFE

1. Great horned owl
2. Mountain lion
3. Syringa (state flower)
4. Mountain bluebird (state bird)
5. California quail
6. Ring-necked pheasant
7. Mountain goat
8. Moose
9. Swainson's hawk
10. Rainbow trout
11. Pika
12. Dark-eyed junco
13. Mallards
14. Golden eagle
15. Rocky Mountain elk
16. Lewis's woodpecker
17. Mule deer
18. Collared lizard
19. Pacific tree frog
20. Sage grouse
21. Pronghorn

ABOUT THE ART...

A poster of this art is available from the Idaho Watchable Wildlife Committee. Proceeds from the sales will benefit future reprints of the Idaho Wildlife Viewing Guide and Idaho's Watchable Wildlife Program. Contact the Idaho Department of Fish and Game at 208/334-2920 for more information.

TABLE OF CONTENTS

IDAHO STATE MAP

Idaho's wildlife viewing sites have been organized into seven regions, using the names adopted by the Idaho Department of Travel and Tourism. Each region is introduced by a regional map showing major roads and cities, as well as the location of each wildlife viewing site. Each region is also color-coded by easy-find strips along the page edges of this guide. The wildlife viewing sites are numbered consecutively from north to south for easier reference.

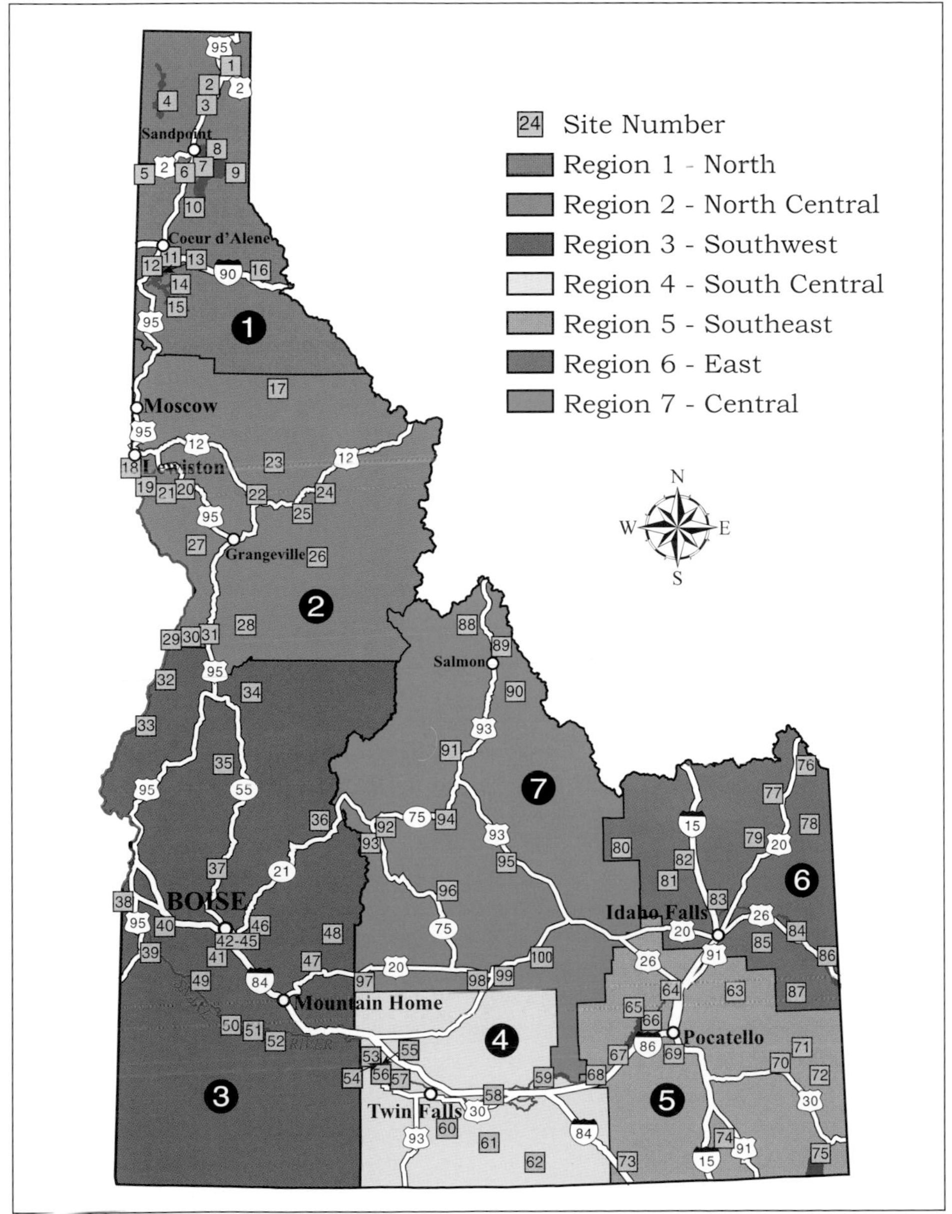

INTRODUCTION

Idaho is a state rich in numbers and diversity of wildlife with 357 bird, 109 mammal, 22 reptile, 15 amphibian, and 68 fish species. Wildlife occupy vast expanses of uncrowded, unspoiled natural areas, as much of the state is public land and Idaho's population is relatively low.

This guide will direct you to the best wildlife viewing opportunities in Idaho. It is designed for both the casual and experienced wildlife viewer, for planning specific viewing trips, or simply carrying in your car to help you find wildlife as you travel. Idaho has outstanding scenic wonders that provide great wildlife viewing opportunities.

Mojave black-collared lizard
© Colleen Sweeney

NATIONAL WATCHABLE WILDLIFE PROGRAM

The increased public interest in wildlife viewing led to a U.S. Watchable Wildlife Initiative of 1990. Fourteen governmental agencies and conservation organizations cooperate to promote conservation, recreation, and education through wildlife viewing programs. Nature tourists can pick up wildlife viewing guides for 41 states and three Canadian provinces. The mission of the Watchable Wildlife Program is to enhance, elevate, and promote wildlife viewing and nature appreciation for the benefit of society, while building community awareness, understanding, and support for the conservation of the wildlife and habitats upon which these activities depend.

RESPONSIBLE VIEWING AND OUTDOOR ETHICS

Most birders, wildlife photographers, sportsmen, and others who venture outdoors share a genuine appreciation of wildlife. Unintentionally, wildlife watchers can harm wildlife through direct disturbance, feeding the animals, littering, or disobeying laws. People may place themselves in danger by approaching wildlife too closely or may spoil the viewing experience of others. The following guidelines will help avoid harm to people and wildlife:

- **Minimize disturbances to wildlife**. Allow animals to carry out their normal behavior without interruption. Watch for subtle signs of distress such as head raised, ears pointed in direction of the observers, skittish movements, or alarm calls. Animals are very sensitive to human presence and will flee if approached too closely. This leads to animals using valuable energy at a time when they may already be stressed by winter cold or limited food supplies, abandoning eggs or young that need to be kept warm and protected from predators, or injuring themselves in the process of fleeing.

- Use quiet, slow movements to avoid startling wildlife. A car or boat makes a great blind in which to hide yourself, and you may actually see more by remaining in it.

- Keep far enough away from nests and dens to avoid disturbing breeding wildlife.

- Never chase, repeatedly flush, or attempt to capture animals. Harassing animals is punishable by state and federal laws.

- Do not pick up sick or orphaned animals. You should phone the local IDFG conservation officer to evaluate a distressed animal properly.

- **Obey posted rules**. Many of the sites in this book have rules posted that explain when and where people can go. Some of these rules are designed to avoid disturbing wildlife during important periods such as the breeding season.

  - Observe road closed signs. Closures give animals space to prevent being disturbed by vehicle traffic.

  - Always obtain permission from landowners before entering private property.

- **Never feed wildlife**. Animals accustomed to being fed by or being close to humans have a good chance of being hit by a car, ingesting plastic and other litter, starving to death when that food source is no longer present, or becoming a nuisance and having to be removed from the area.

- **Keep pets leashed**. Do not allow them to chase or harass wildlife.

- **Avoid dangerous wildlife**. Always keep a good distance between yourself and rattlesnakes, bears with cubs, rutting elk and moose, and moose with calves. These animals may charge if threatened and can inflict serious injury.
If entering grizzly bear country, talk to the local management agency and familiarize yourself with bear safety.

- **Respect the rights of others**. Be considerate when approaching wildlife already under observation by other viewers or photographers.

VIEWING HINTS

- The most important equipment for wildlife viewing is a pair of binoculars. Higher powered spotting telescopes are useful in areas where the wildlife is expected to be a good distance away, but may be too heavy to carry on long hikes. Field guides can greatly enhance the experience, especially if you are learning wildlife identification.

- Each wildlife species in Idaho has different daily and seasonal activity periods. Typically, the best time of the day to view wildlife is when they are feeding, usually in the early morning and late afternoon. The best seasons for seeing large numbers of wildlife, especially birds, are during the spring and fall migrations. Wetlands, lakes, rivers, marshes, and mudflats are good places to look for wildlife. In winter, look for open water as animals, especially waterfowl and wading birds, congregate in these areas. Foothills at the base of mountain ranges can harbor hoofed mammals such as elk, deer, and pronghorn that move downslope to avoid poor foraging conditions in the deep snow.

- Awareness of habitats is a valuable tool for wildlife watchers. Simply stated, an animal's habitat is where the creature lives. Habitat provides the four basics for survival: food, water, shelter, and space. Within a habitat type, special features may be required so that a particular species can even occupy the area. Important features might include snags (dead, standing trees), logs, rocky cliff areas, a stream or water source, a burrow in the ground, or a cave. Looking for these types of habitat features when you visit the viewing sites will help you to spot wildlife.

- Some types of animals live only in very few kinds of habitats and are called specialists. Generalists, on the other hand, thrive in a variety of habitats. Because there are so many wildlife species in Idaho, it would be impossible to list all of those that occur at each site. By becoming familiar with Idaho's habitats and the different species that live in them, you can predict what you will likely see at a particular site. By doing a little pre-trip planning, you can avoid the disappointment of not seeing much wildlife.

ALPINE FOREST ECOSYSTEM

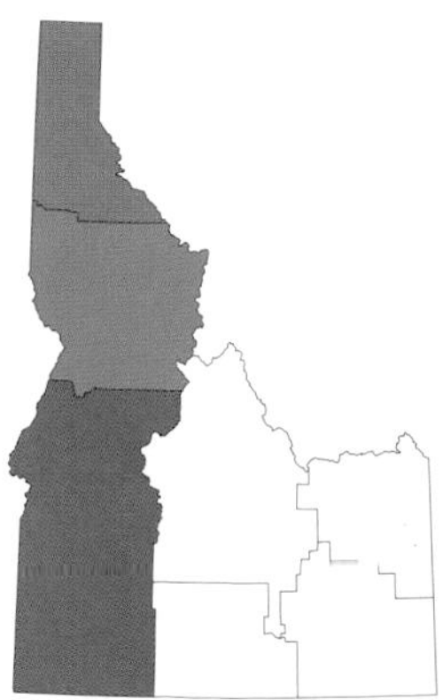

Alpine forests cover much of Idaho's high-elevation areas over 9,000 feet. "Above-treeline" forests can include rock or talus slopes but also are interspersed with wildflower-laden meadows. This land of high sun and wind has few trees and very low shrubs that provide excellent habitat for large mammals such as mountain goats. An occasional marmot, golden-mantled ground squirrel, or pika may scurry across the land, while the Clark's nutcracker, Townsend's solitaire and black rosy-finch flit about. The bright lapis-colored mountain bluebird may be seen in alpine forest areas, but they do not breed in such harsh, high country. Mountain lakes may also harbor spotted frogs and long-toed salamanders.

GRASSLAND ECOSYSTEM

Idaho's northern ecosystem is often referred to as the "Palouse Country." Prairie and canyon grassland areas are fertile grounds for plant species such as Idaho fescue, sego lily, Sandberg's bluegrass, yarrow, and the colorful lupine and camas. White-tailed deer, mule deer, bobcat, and black-tailed jackrabbit are the primary mammals in this ecosystem. Distinctive Idaho prairieland birds include the western meadowlark, sharp-tailed grouse, bobolink, northern harrier, and barn owl. Harvest mice dine on bountiful grasshoppers while fence lizards and painted turtles amble along.

CONIFEROUS FOREST ECOSYSTEM

Coniferous forests/woodlands are characteristic of Idaho's sweeping high-to-low elevation forests. Fir and spruce trees are most commonly found at elevations of 8,000–9,000 feet. As elevation drops, subalpine species such as lodgepole pines begin to appear. The lowest elevations support yellow pine and ponderosa pine. Black bear dine on huckleberries, and elk feed in meadows on grasses and other vegetation. The mighty mountain lion (cougar) prefers the high, rocky ledges of this ecosystem. The hollow knocking sound of pileated and Lewis's woodpeckers is common in coniferous forests. Red-tailed chipmunks, northern flying squirrels, and voles scamper amidst the forest under the close watch of sharp-shinned hawks. A visit to this ecosystem would not be complete without a glimpse of the western toad or wood frog.

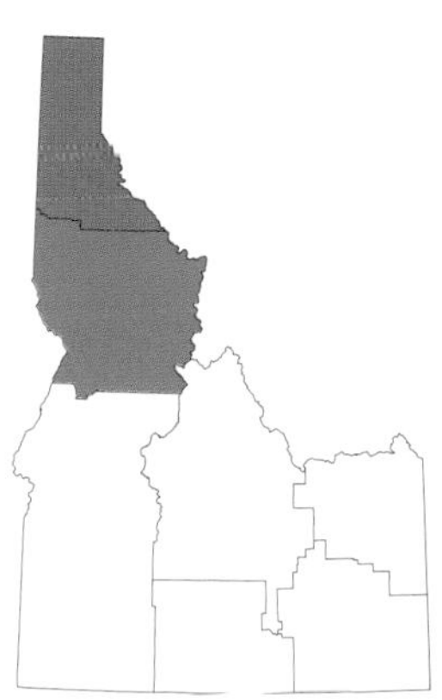

RIPARIAN ECOSYSTEM

Riparian (wetland) areas are scattered throughout Idaho, most commonly found in thin strips of lush, green vegetation near rivers, streams, lakes, ponds, and marshes. These "ribbons of green" are often comprised of willow, dogwood, and wild rose under cottonwood overstories. Marsh cattails, pond cattails, and sedges waver in the breeze while red-winged blackbirds and yellow warblers balance upon them for a moment's rest. The bald eagle and great blue heron wait patiently for a tasty dinner of trout while the mighty moose, river otter, and beaver busily explore the riparian territory. Waterfowl abounds in wetlands including mallards, teal, and wood ducks. Frogs, salamanders, and garter snakes, amidst insects such as dragonflies and mayflies, complete one of Idaho's most complex ecosystems.

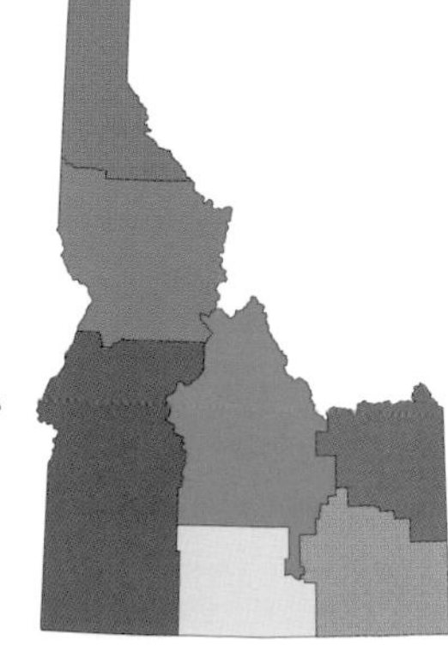

URBAN ECOSYSTEM

Idaho is one of the fastest growing states in the nation. Urban wildlife is found in nearly every corner of Idaho because of yard irrigation or proximity to rivers. All types of exotic trees, flowers, bushes, and grasses create a special ecosystem—although arguably manmade. Raccoons, skunks, fox, and introduced squirrels curiously roam neighborhoods while the familiar robin, magpie, and introduced starlings and house sparrows take to nesting on, and even in, our homes. When near neighborhood ponds, don't forget to listen for the distinctive low bellow of the bullfrog.

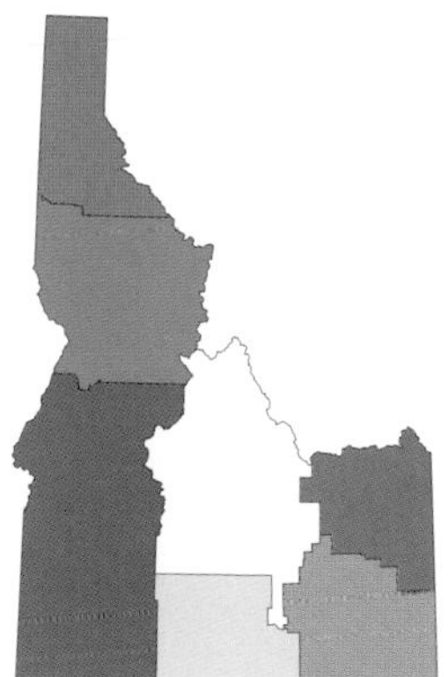

SHRUB–STEPPE ECOSYSTEM

In this arid country of the Snake River Plain and at lower elevations across the central Idaho Batholith, sagebrush and bunchgrasses dominate the terrain. Nearly one-half of southern Idaho is considered shrub-steppe habitat, which is an integral part of the Great Basin Desert. In other areas such as the Owyhee Uplands, pine and juniper dominate the landscape. Mammals most often found include pronghorn, badger, coyote, Paiute ground squirrel, and mountain cottontail. Birds such as sage thrasher, horned lark, western scrub-jay, sage grouse, ferruginous hawk, and burrowing owl prefer the drier shrub-steppe ecosystem. Keep an eye to the ground as rattlesnakes, gopher snakes, and sagebrush lizards often surprise visitors.

AGRICULTURAL ECOSYSTEM

Much of Idaho's land is devoted to many different types of agriculture. Idaho's croplands and pastures support potatoes, wheat, corn, alfalfa, and soybeans. Some trees and shrubs occur between fields and provide forage or prey for various animals. Fox, deer, coyote, yellow-bellied marmots, and pocket gophers call croplands and pastures home. Crows, ravens, magpies, cowbirds, and long-billed curlews often search on the ground for food, while raptors, such as the Swainson's hawk, circle above searching for potential prey. The very colorful ring-necked pheasant can be a treat to see on the edge of Idaho's agricultural fields.

HOW TO USE THIS BOOK

The color strips on the outside of the pages are keyed to each of the seven travel regions in Idaho. The sites are numbered consecutively from 1 to 100. Maps of each region with the site numbers are at the beginning of each section. Additional detailed maps are located within a page of the site information. The *Description* has information about the area, habitats, and scenic values. *Viewing Information* describes specific places to view wildlife and lists some species found at the site. Only unique or representative species are listed.

Species symbols are limited to seven per site and indicate either the species most likely to be present or those unique to the area. Many sites have the Important Bird Area (IBA) symbol. IBAs are sites that provide essential habitat for one or more species of bird and are designated by Idaho Partners in Flight. The IBA program provides science-based priorities for habitat conservation and promotes positive action to safeguard vital bird habitats.

Site Notes include roads not listed on the map and gives additional information on where to get more detailed maps and species lists. *Contact Information* signifies the best agency or entity to contact if you have questions concerning individual sites. The names of private owners or organizations are not always listed. Private sites have been included in the book only with the permission of the owners. Please respect their rights when visiting these sites. The phone number listed is usually the managing agency or organization.

Facility symbols are listed only if they are on the site. In some cases, restrooms or hotels may be nearby. The barrier-free symbol is used at sites that have universally-accessible trails or interpretive facilities. Recreational symbols are listed to indicate various opportunities at each site that are conducive to wildlife watching. The managing agency can provide information on other types of recreational activities at the sites. Season symbols indicate the time of year the site is open to visitors or the best seasons to view wildlife.

SYMBOLS

BLM—U.S. Bureau of Land Management
BOR—U.S. Bureau of Reclamation
IDFG—Idaho Department of Fish and Game
IDPR—Idaho Department of Parks and Recreation
ITD—Idaho Transportation Department
NPS—National Park Service
PVT—Privately owned land
USFWS—U.S. Fish and Wildlife Service
USFS—U.S. Forest Service

FEATURED WILDLIFE

Songbirds, Perching Birds — Upland Birds — Shorebirds — Raptors, Birds of Prey — Aquatic Birds — Wading Birds

Waterfowl — Freshwater Mammals — Fish — Reptiles, Amphibians — Bats

Hoofed Mammals — Carnivores — Small Mammals — Insects — Wildflowers — Important Bird Area

FACILITIES AND RECREATION

Parking — Restrooms Pit Toilets — Barrier-Free — Picnic Area — Drinking Water — Hiking

Entry Fee — Camping — Bicycling — Cross-Country Skiing — Horse Trails — Non-motorized Boats

Lodging — Restaurants — Boat Ramp — Motorized Boats

BEST VIEWING SEASONS

Spring — Summer — Fall — Winter

HIGHWAY SIGNS

The Watchable Wildlife binocular signs identify the route to wildlife viewing sites.

Coeur d'Alene Lake © George Wuerthner

REGION ONE

NORTH

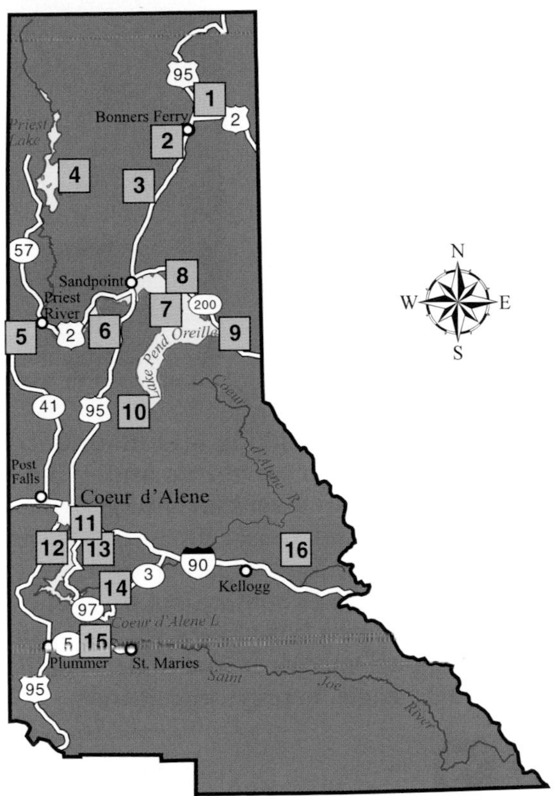

WILDLIFE VIEWING SITES

1 Purcell Mountains Area
2 Kootenai National Wildlife Refuge
3 McArthur Wildlife Management Area
4 Priest Lake Area
5 Albeni Falls Dam and Vicinity
6 Round Lake State Park
7 Gamlin Lake Preserve
8 Lake Pend Oreille – Pack River Delta
9 Lake Pend Oreille – Clark Fork River Delta/Fish Hatchery
10 Farragut State Park
11 Coeur d'Alene Lake – Tubbs Hill Nature Park
12 Coeur d'Alene Lake – Cougar Bay
13 Coeur d'Alene Lake – Wolf Lodge Bay
14 Coeur d'Alene River – Chain of Lakes/Old Mission State Park
15 Heyburn State Park
16 Settler's Grove of Ancient Cedars

1 PURCELL MOUNTAINS AREA

Copper Falls in the Purcell Mountains
© George Wuerthner

DESCRIPTION: This scenic route through the Purcell Mountains leads you to four mountain lakes, past a prairie marsh, along the Moyie River, and up to an alpine lake.

VIEWING INFORMATION: The lower lakes offer good opportunities to view moose, wood duck, common golden-eye, mergansers, and osprey. While driving by Round Prairie, a marshy meadow along U.S. 95, look for waterfowl and wading birds. Take the short loop trails from the Robinson Lake day use area to view a heron rookery and osprey nest. Meadow Creek Campground has hiking and mountain bike trails along the Moyie River; look for riparian songbirds and white-tailed deer. Queen Lake is a high mountain lake with moose, boreal chickadees, and boreal owls. Although owls are not likely to be seen, at night they may respond to imitated calls. Most of the lakes have camping and/or day use areas, fishing, and small boating opportunities. A side trip to Perkins Lake features a floating boardwalk with interpretive signs describing the unique plant species in the area. Wildlife species include common goldeneye, bald eagle, osprey, and moose.

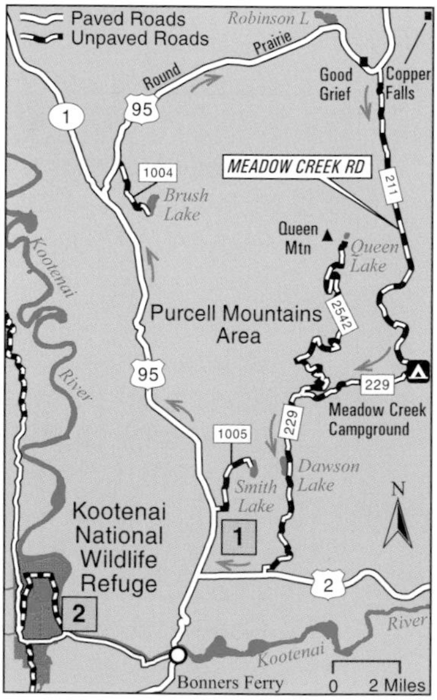

SITE NOTES: Roads are not maintained in winter; the best viewing is from late spring through fall. If time permits, visit the scenic Copper Falls, which features a loop trail that is universally accessible. The turnoff for the falls is 3 miles north of Good Grief.

CONTACT INFORMATION: USFS (208/267-5561), The Nature Conservancy (208/676-8176), and PVT

SIZE: 45+ mile loop

CLOSEST TOWN: Bonners Ferry

2 KOOTENAI NATIONAL WILDLIFE REFUGE

DESCRIPTION: The wide variety of habitats in this scenic refuge support abundant and diverse wildlife. Meadows are interspersed with grain fields and wetlands in the valley bottom adjacent to the Kootenai River. Wetlands feature open-water ponds, cattail marshes, tree-lined ponds, and rushing creeks. A small portion of the refuge ascends the foothills of the densely forested Selkirk Mountains.

VIEWING INFORMATION: Approximately 220 bird and 45 mammal species are found on the refuge. Tundra swans, Canada geese, and ducks are most abundant during spring and fall migrations. Common summertime birds include the great blue heron, Canada goose, ruffed grouse, osprey, northern harrier, great horned owl, and numerous songbirds. Bald eagles, which nest on the refuge, and rough-legged hawks are present in higher numbers from November through March. Look for elk, deer, moose, beaver, coyote, and black bear during fall and spring, especially in the morning and evening hours. View the refuge via a 4.5-mile auto tour or from 5.5 miles of walking trails. A wildlife viewing blind is located about 0.25 mile past the refuge office. There are mountain biking trails to the west of the refuge; check with the USFS for best routes. Refuge use is restricted during fall waterfowl hunting season on Tuesdays, Thursdays, and weekends.

SITE NOTES: See map on page 24. The refuge office (open Monday through Friday) is two miles beyond the entrance. Brochures, maps, and a wildlife checklist are available at the office and at several sites on the refuge.

CONTACT INFORMATION: USFWS (208/267-3888)

SIZE: 2,774 acres

CLOSEST TOWN: Bonners Ferry

White-tailed ptarmigan © Gary Kramer

3 McARTHUR WILDLIFE MANAGEMENT AREA

DESCRIPTION: This WMA, with 600 acres of marshy lake surrounded by very scenic coniferous forest, was the state's first land acquisition for waterfowl production. The area also serves as an important corridor for wildlife traveling between the Selkirks and the Cabinet Mountains.

VIEWING INFORMATION: McArthur Lake hosts hundreds of tundra swans and Canada geese and thousands of ducks and American coots through spring and fall migrations. Lesser numbers of black terns, Virginia rails, red-necked grebes, and marsh wrens also occur. Other species to look for include bald eagle, osprey, and great blue heron. In June, moose frequently feed in the lake in the early morning. Shorebirds are common along the west shore in August. Hunting and fishing are popular; boating is allowed from July 1 to March 15.

SITE NOTES: A brochure is available at the IDFG office in Coeur d'Alene.

CONTACT INFORMATION: IDFG (208/263-6004 or 769-1414)

SIZE: 1,200 acres

CLOSEST TOWN: Naples

Woodland caribou found in the Priest Lake Area
© Tom J. Ulrich

4 PRIEST LAKE AREA

Priest Lake © George Wuerthner

DESCRIPTION: This large, pristine lake is surrounded by densely forested mountains, the Selkirk Range.

VIEWING INFORMATION: The Selkirks provide habitat for small numbers of the federally endangered grizzly bear, woodland caribou, and bull trout. Follow the rugged roads from either of the two state park units (Indian Creek or Lionhead) east into the mountains where you may see white-tailed deer, moose, black bear, coyote, and sometimes mountain goat. The uncommon harlequin duck, which nests along fast-flowing streams, can be found in the Priest River drainage. Numerous hiking trails and scenic vistas are found on both sides of the lake; interpretive sites and the Hanna Flats Interpretive Trail are located on the west side of the lake.

SITE NOTES: USFS maps are available at the Priest Lake Ranger Station on the lake's west side; maps of the east side are available from the Department of Lands office at Cavanaugh Bay or at Indian Creek Park Store. Brochures and guided walks are available at Indian Creek and Lionhead Campgrounds, Memorial Day to Labor Day (call ahead for other times).

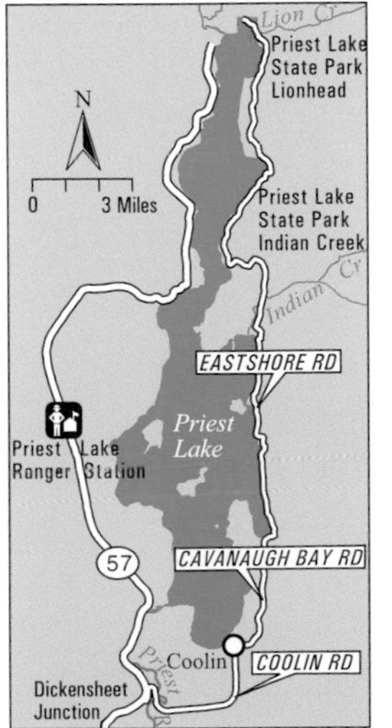

CONTACT INFORMATION: IDPR (208/443-2200), USFS (208/443-2512)

SIZE: IDPR 713 acres; FS 4,000 acres

CLOSEST TOWN: Coolin

5 ALBENI FALLS DAM AND VICINITY

DESCRIPTION: Albeni Falls Dam retains scenic Lake Pend Oreille and 25 miles of the Pend Oreille River. Recreational sites along the river contain a variety of wildlife habitats, offering many viewing opportunities.

VIEWING INFORMATION: From the Vista Area or powerhouse parking lot, look upstream to the railroad bridge supporting several osprey and Canada goose nests. Look for waterfowl on both sides of the dam, and scan the trees on the high bluffs for wintering bald eagles. River areas at Albeni Cove, Priest River, and Riley Creek provide habitat for waterfowl and marine birds, best viewed in spring and fall. Muskrats and painted turtles can be seen basking on logs and rocks. Birds of prey can be viewed year-round but white-tailed deer and moose are best seen in winter. Songbirds are commonly found in the forested areas. Bear and elk also frequent the area. Recreation facilities are accessible by foot year-round, but open to vehicle traffic from May through September only.

SITE NOTES: Maps are available at the Vista Area. U.S. 2 between Sandpoint and Newport offers excellent opportunities to view wildlife year-round.

CONTACT INFORMATION: ACE (208/437-3133)

SIZE: 13 miles of river

CLOSEST TOWN: Priest River

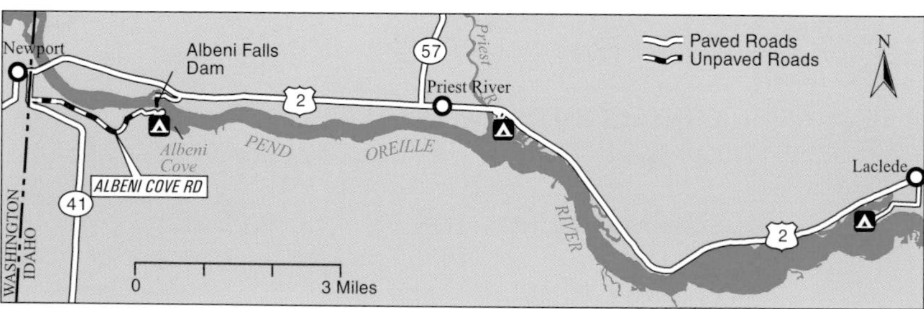

6 ROUND LAKE STATE PARK

Mountain bluebird © Gary Kramer

DESCRIPTION: This 58-acre, glacially-created, pothole lake is encircled by coniferous forest. A foot trail around the lake and along Cocolalla Creek takes you under canopies of western white pine, Engelmann spruce, grand fir, lodgepole pine, black cottonwood, paper birch, red alder, and Rocky Mountain maple.

VIEWING INFORMATION: The lake supports nesting osprey and great blue heron, beaver, muskrat, mink, and a few species of amphibians and reptiles. While exploring the park's trails, you may see white-tailed deer, raccoons, and red squirrels. Numerous bird species include northern flicker, pileated woodpecker, barn and tree swallows, gray and Steller's jays, mountain bluebird, cedar waxwing, and western tanager. A self-guided botanical trail includes a view of the state flower, the syringa, which blooms in late June. Wildlife can be observed year-round, although spring and fall are best. Ducks and geese use the lake until late winter, when cross-country skiing is possible. For additional viewing, the Morton Slough area, where Cocolalla Creek joins Lake Pend Oreille, has shallow marshes that provide great habitat for waterfowl and songbirds. Osprey, bald eagles (in winter), and golden eagles are often seen in this area.

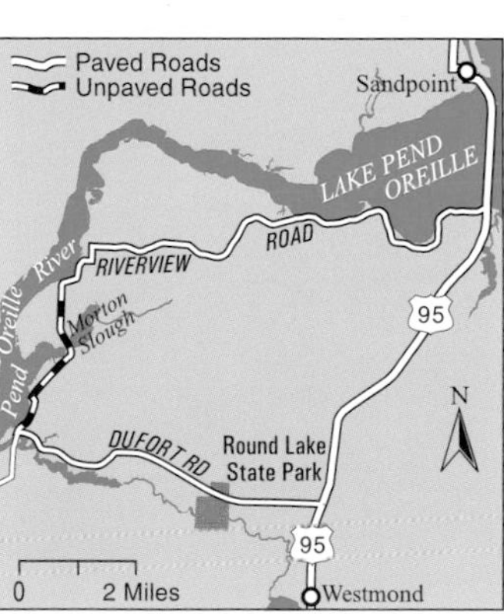

CONTACT INFORMATION: IDPR (208/263-3489)

SIZE: 200 acres

CLOSEST TOWN: Westmond

7 GAMLIN LAKE PRESERVE

DESCRIPTION: Gamlin Lake, located at the northern end of Lake Pend Oreille, has a diversely vegetated shoreline, wetlands, and good waterfowl habitat. A fairly moist, coniferous forest surrounds the lake.

VIEWING INFORMATION: In addition to waterfowl, check for common yellowthroats and red-winged blackbirds. Amphibians include spotted and wood frogs. The forest sustains western red cedar, western hemlock, grand fir, western larch, and Douglas fir and supports at least 27 nesting bird species, including the pileated woodpecker and Swainson's thrush. Mammals include beaver, black bear, white-tailed deer, and elk. Enjoy wildlife and wildflower viewing, fishing, kayaking, canoeing, hiking, and a serene atmosphere.

SITE NOTES: Follow Glengary Bay Road along the lake for about one mile to the parking area, where trails can be accessed. The boat launch is located off Glengary Bay Road, about a half mile before the parking area.

CONTACT INFORMATION: The Nature Conservancy (208/676-8176), BLM (208/769-5000)

SIZE: 401 acres

CLOSEST TOWN: Sagle

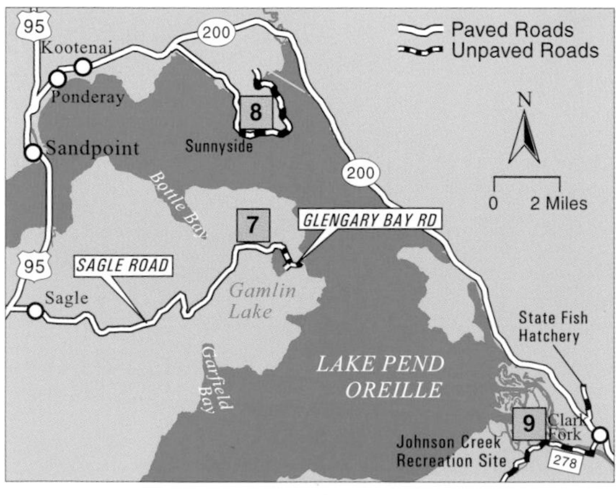

Spotted frog © Janice Engle

8 LAKE PEND OREILLE — PACK RIVER DELTA

DESCRIPTION: Lake Pend Oreille, measuring 43 miles long and over 1,000 feet deep, is completely encircled by mountains and bordered by several wildlife management areas and undeveloped public land.

VIEWING INFORMATION: The lake becomes a haven for wildlife during fall and spring; wildlife is less abundant during summer and winter. In the delta, look for waterfowl (including Pacific, red-throated, and common loons), white-tailed deer, moose, beaver, and muskrat. Osprey, bald eagles, and great blue herons nest along the shoreline. In a slough on the west side of the highway bridge, moose are so frequently seen that the state highway department has installed special caution signs.

SITE NOTES: See map on page 30. There are two access points to the Pack River area. A more detailed map is available at the USFS office in Sandpoint.

CONTACT INFORMATION: ACE, managed by IDFG (208/769-1414)

SIZE: 8-mile route

CLOSEST TOWN: Sandpoint

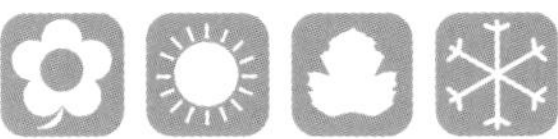

Common loon © Idaho Department of Fish and Game

9 LAKE PEND OREILLE — CLARK FORK RIVER DELTA/FISH HATCHERY

Cutthroat trout © William H. Mullins

DESCRIPTION: This is one of northern Idaho's best areas for viewing waterfowl, osprey, bald eagles, and shorebirds. The Clark Fork River Delta is a mixture of cottonwood riparian forest, open water, grassland, small lakeshore wetlands, and exposed mudflats.

VIEWING INFORMATION: High numbers of waterfowl, shorebirds, and songbirds are present during spring and fall migrations. Look for redheads, wood ducks, and tundra swans. More than 20 osprey pairs and several great blue herons nest in the vicinity, which is also an important wintering area for hundreds of bald eagles. Elk, white-tailed deer, and moose are common. The Clark Fork Hatchery offers guided tours seven days a week, featuring several fish species. Most species are on-site in summer, while cutthroat and kamloops are also present in winter. In the creek next to the hatchery, you may view wild kamloops spawning in April or wild kokanee spawning in November and December. The hatchery area also has nesting osprey, wintering bald eagles, white-tailed deer, and moose. Often a dipper (a bird of fast flowing streams) may be seen in the creek nearby; wood ducks and river otters are also common residents of the area.

SITE NOTES: See map on page 30. There are no developed trails, but you can walk along the dirt spurs into marshy areas. Canoeing is the best way to explore the delta but should only be done outside the spring nesting season. A paddling guide for the Clark Fork Delta is available at IDFG. The campground at Johnson Creek is undeveloped.

CONTACT INFORMATION: IDFG (208/266-1141 or 769-1414), ACE (208/437-3133), PVT

SIZE: Seven miles of river **CLOSEST TOWN:** Clark Fork

10 FARRAGUT STATE PARK

Mountain goats © Gary Kramer

DESCRIPTION: This park offers scenic views of tall-forested mountains, steep rugged cliffs, and Lake Pend Oreille.

VIEWING INFORMATION: Mountain goats, a unique wildlife attraction, roam the steep cliffs of Bernard Peak. The park has an interpretive sign about the goats and a spotting scope for public use at the Willow Picnic Area. The easiest way to view goats is with binoculars from the lakeshore. For a closer look, you can approach the cliffs by boat. The goats have become accustomed to boats and will not flee if you remain quiet in your boat. Park trails lead through forest habitat where white-tailed deer, red squirrels, Columbian ground squirrels, chipmunks, ravens, and songbirds are common. Black bear, mountain lion, bobcat, and coyote are also present, though rarely seen.

SITE NOTES: Stop by the visitor center and pick up a detailed park map and view the nature, interpretive, and historical displays.

CONTACT INFORMATION: IDPR (208/683-2425), IDFG

SIZE: 4,000 acres

CLOSEST TOWN: Bayview

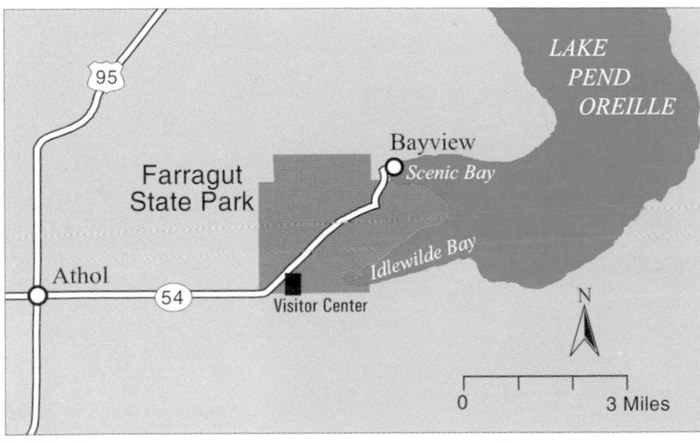

11 COEUR D'ALENE LAKE — TUBBS HILL NATURE PARK

DESCRIPTION: Tubbs Hill is a forested peninsula that extends nearly a mile and a half into picturesque Coeur d'Alene Lake and features numerous trails. The main trail begins at the public boat launch on the peninsula's west side. It follows the shoreline for 1.4 miles to Tubbs point and continues by caves, beaches, scenic overlooks, and side trails that head over the hilltop. A suspension bridge along the trail spans a small gorge. Exit the trail at the marina, or continue to McEuen Playfield, near the boat launch area.

VIEWING INFORMATION: This site is great for watching numerous forest songbirds. In summer look for red-breasted nuthatch, Steller's and gray jays, evening and black-headed grosbeaks, and black-capped, mountain, and chestnut-backed chickadees. In winter, watch for pine siskin, dark-eyed junco, red crossbill, and downy woodpecker. Commonly sighted lake birds are osprey, common merganser, and pied-billed grebe in summer and bald eagle, hooded merganser, and horned, eared, and western grebes in winter.

SITE NOTES: The main trailhead begins at the launch and ends at McEuen Playfield. A mapboard at the trailhead shows all the trails. A trail booklet is available at the City Park office on Fifth Street (near the playfield). The city of Coeur d'Alene has all facilities and is within easy walking distance.

CONTACT INFORMATION: City of Coeur d'Alene (208/769-2252), PVT

SIZE: 150 acres, two miles of shoreline

CLOSEST TOWN:
Coeur d'Alene

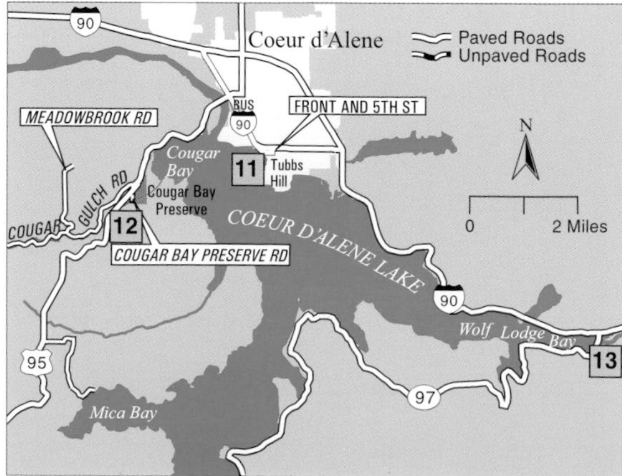

12 COEUR D'ALENE LAKE — COUGAR BAY

Bald eagle © Gary Kramer

DESCRIPTION: The shallow Cougar Bay is rich with aquatic vegetation and bordered by marshland, coniferous forest, and fields that attract abundant wildlife.

VIEWING INFORMATION: During fall and spring migration, the bays are filled with waterfowl including tundra swan, Canada goose, wood duck, blue-winged and cinnamon teal, northern shoveler, ruddy duck, and mallard. Bald eagles are common in winter. Summer breeding birds include osprey, great blue heron, sora, killdeer, spotted sandpiper, Wilson's snipe, mountain bluebird, violet-green swallow, cinnamon teal, and red-necked, pied-billed, and western grebes. A bald eagle pair nests in the area. Western toads and Pacific tree frogs croak loudly at night. The proximity of forest and farmland provides habitat year-round for songbirds, including warblers, chickadees, flycatchers, and woodpeckers, along with raptors, elk, deer, coyote, and black bear.

SITE NOTES: See map on page 34. Interpretive trails lead from the wetlands to the forested areas. Canoe access is available at Cougar Beach (BLM property 1.5 miles south of the Spokane River bridge). Also stop at Mica Bay for more viewing.

CONTACT INFORMATION: The Nature Conservancy (208/676-8176), PVT

SIZE: 226 acres

CLOSEST TOWN: Coeur d'Alene

   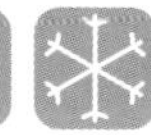     

13 COEUR D'ALENE LAKE — WOLF LODGE BAY

DESCRIPTION: Wolf Lodge Bay attracts up to 60 migratory bald eagles when the lake's kokanee salmon spawn and die during November and December. The surrounding steep mountain slopes, covered with dense stands of western larch, Douglas fir, ponderosa pine, and grand fir provide excellent communal roosting perches for the eagles.

VIEWING INFORMATION: Good viewing areas are at Higgins Point, Mineral Ridge Boat Launch, and Mineral Ridge Trailhead. Peak bald eagle populations occur from mid-December to January 1st; by mid-January most eagles have dispersed from the area. Bald eagles are sensitive to human disturbance, especially when approached by foot; use your boat or car for a viewing blind. Spring and summer visitors can take a three-mile loop nature trail at Mineral Ridge to see songbirds. Marshy areas at the mouths of Wolf Lodge and Blue Creeks are also good birding spots—view from the road only. Try an additional hiking trail (FS 257) off Beauty Creek. From September to November, view migrating chinook salmon from the frontage road bridge over Wolf Lodge Creek just north of the Interstate 90 bridge crossing.

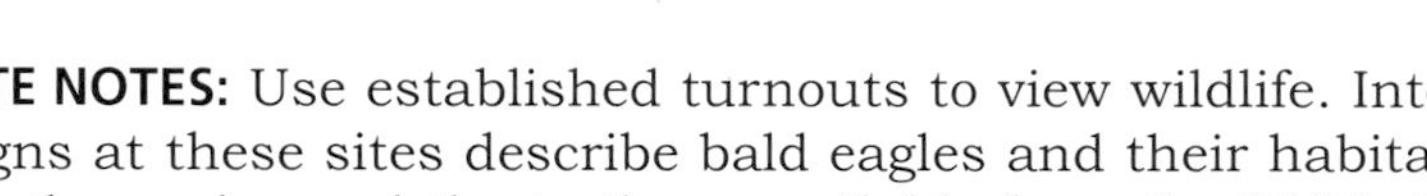

SITE NOTES: Use established turnouts to view wildlife. Interpretive signs at these sites describe bald eagles and their habitat. Brochures on the eagles and the trail are available from the BLM office at 1808 N. Third Street in Coeur d'Alene.

CONTACT INFORMATION: BLM (208/765-1511), PVT

SIZE: 900 acres

CLOSEST TOWN: Coeur d'Alene

   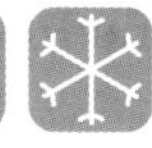

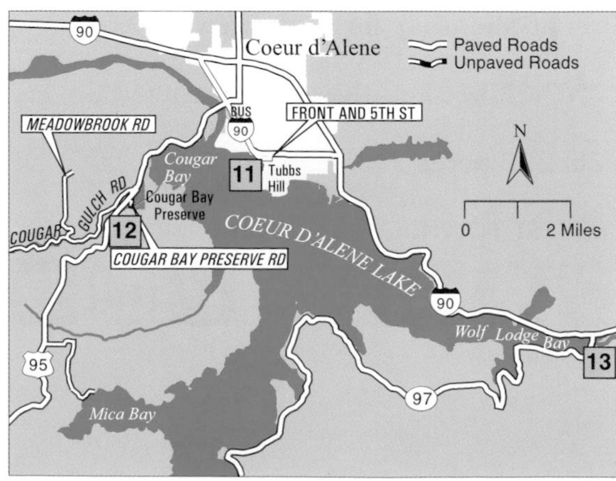

14 COEUR D'ALENE RIVER — CHAIN OF LAKES/ OLD MISSION STATE PARK

Coeur d'Alene River © Leland Howard

DESCRIPTION: This 13-mile stretch of the Coeur d'Alene River is bordered by numerous shallow lakes and marshy wetlands—an excellent area for canoeing. Adjacent mountain slopes are thickly covered with coniferous trees and dense shrubby undergrowth. An additional viewing area is Old Mission State Park, which sits atop a high knoll and features the oldest standing building in Idaho.

VIEWING INFORMATION: Ducks, Canada geese, and tundra swans are numerous, particularly during migration, and this river stretch is a major breeding area for tree cavity-nesting wood ducks. Osprey, great blue heron, American kestrel, red-tailed hawk, belted kingfisher, and several swallow species are also visible. Muskrat and beaver lodges dot the marshlands, and elk and white-tailed deer can be seen in the early morning and evening hours. Fishing and hunting are popular area activities. A viewing blind at Thompson Lake gives outstanding views of the wetlands and wildlife in the area, especially waterfowl, wading birds, and raptors. Some facilities are available at Killarney and Rose Lake. From Old Mission State Park overlooking the Coeur d'Alene River, waterfowl, wading birds, deer, muskrat, and beaver can be seen from spring through fall. Bald eagles use the river area in winter. The park has a short nature trail with interpretive signs.

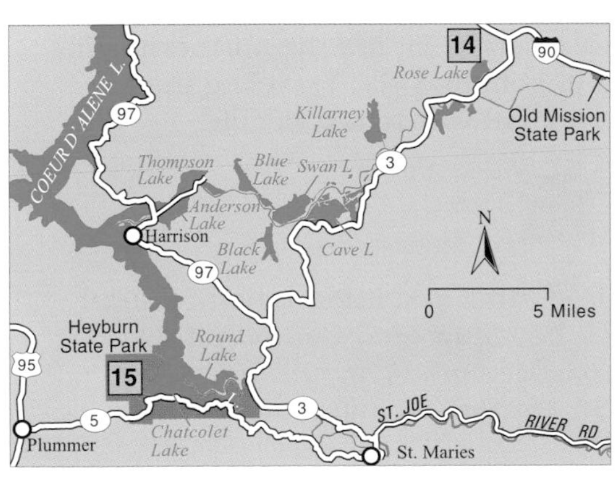

SITE NOTES: Wildlife viewing is from road turnouts, the lake parking areas, or by boat.

CONTACT INFORMATION: IDFG (208/769-1414), USFS, BLM, PVT [Old Mission State Park (208/682-3814)]

SIZE: 13 miles of river **CLOSEST TOWN:** North end—Rose Lake; south end—Harrison

15 HEYBURN STATE PARK

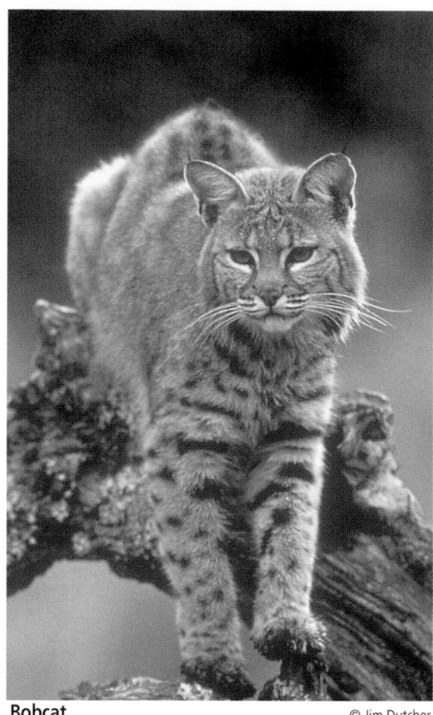
Bobcat © Jim Dutcher

DESCRIPTION: This large, forested state park lies along the south shore of Lake Chatcolet. Here the St. Joe River meanders between two lakes toward Coeur d'Alene Lake.

VIEWING INFORMATION: Extensive marshes and riparian-lined shallow lakes provide important stopover and nesting habitat for waterfowl, great blue heron, and osprey. A key wildlife viewing area is at Plummer Creek Marsh, giving a bird's-eye view of the wetlands. The park hosts over 50 pairs of osprey and, near Benewah Lake, a great blue heron rookery. The park provides osprey, wood duck, and Canada goose nest structures, helping to increase these birds' numbers. The area is also well known for its abundance and diversity of songbird species. A good way to see songbirds is on any of six forested trails (totaling 20 miles), many shaded by 400-year-old ponderosa pines. Mammals commonly seen include the red squirrel, yellowpine chipmunk, snowshoe hare, raccoon, muskrat, beaver, badger, striped skunk, river otter, coyote, white-tailed deer, bobcat, and black bear. Present, but rarely seen, are the northern flying squirrel, marten, wolverine, mountain lion, and elk. Traveling the St. Joe River by canoe or kayak is also a great way to see wildlife.

SITE NOTES: See map on page 37. Brochures and information on local attractions are available at the park headquarters. Campfire programs and guided hikes are conducted from Memorial Day through Labor Day. USFS maps are available in St. Maries, 13 miles east of the park.

CONTACT INFORMATION: IDPR (208/686-1308)

SIZE: 7,838 acres **CLOSEST TOWN:** Plummer

16 SETTLER'S GROVE OF ANCIENT CEDARS

DESCRIPTION: A clear, sparkling stream winds through stands of towering ancient cedar trees. These giants are hundred of years old and have trunks that dwarf the many visitors who walk these trails.

Ancient cedars © Leland Howard

VIEWING INFORMATION: Wildflowers dot the forest floor with shades of pink, yellow, blue, or white. Different flowers may be seen at different times through the summer and fall. Songbirds call out their own tunes while they flit from branch to branch, often out of sight, but not out of listening range. Watch for brown creeper, varied thrush, warblers, chickadees, and woodpeckers. The cool, moist temperatures of this secluded snap shot of history make this site a wonderful place to visit on a hot, dry summer day.

CONTACT INFORMATION: USFS (208/752-1221)

SIZE: 184 acres

CLOSEST TOWN: Murray

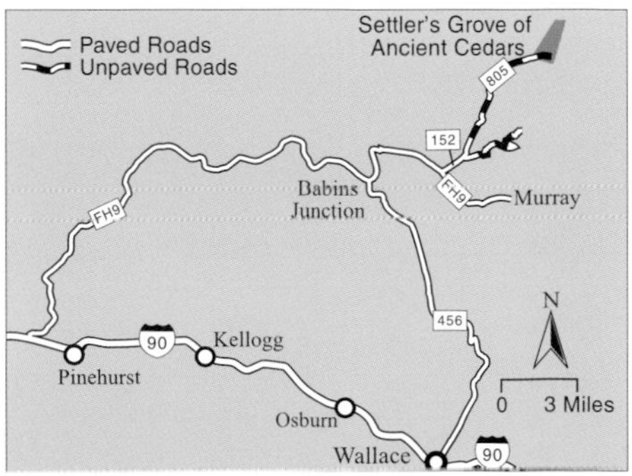

Selway River ©Leland Howard

REGION TWO

NORTH CENTRAL

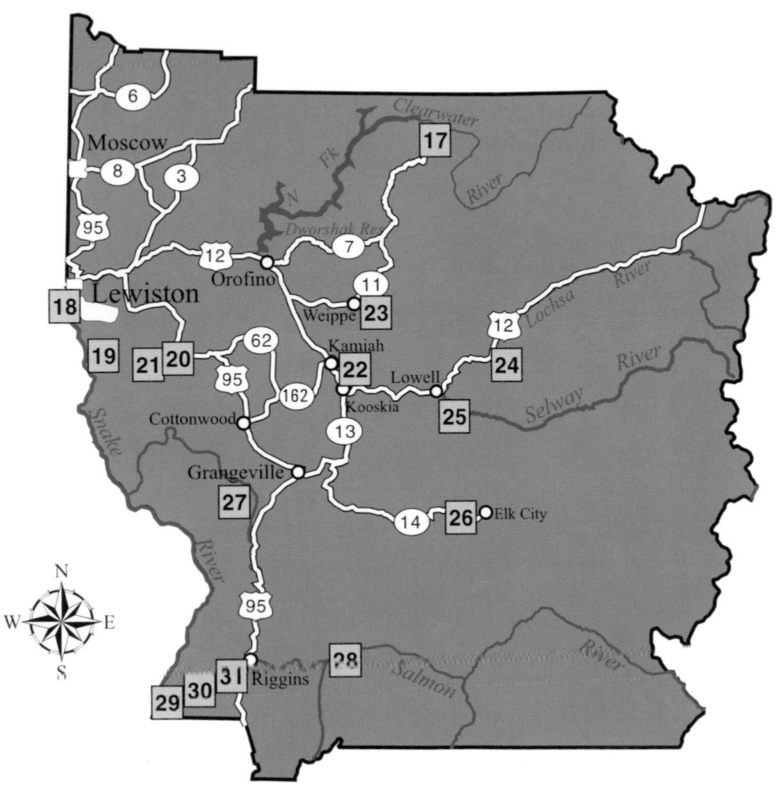

WILDLIFE VIEWING SITES

17 Mallard – Larkins Pioneer Area
18 Hells Gate State Park
19 Craig Mountain Wildlife Management Area
20 Winchester Lake State Park
21 Wolf Education and Research Center
22 Nez Perce National Historical Park – Heart of the Monster Unit
23 Musselshell Meadows
24 Lochsa River Canyon
25 Selway River Canyon
26 Elk City Area/Red River Wildlife Management Area
27 Lower Salmon River Canyon
28 Middle Salmon River Canyon
29 Snake River in Hells Canyon National Recreation Area
30 Seven Devils Mountains in Hells Canyon National Recreation Area
31 Rapid River Fish Hatchery

17 MALLARD — LARKINS PIONEER AREA

Crag Lake in Mallard-Larkins Pioneer Area
© Craig Groves

DESCRIPTION: The Mallard-Larkins Pioneer Area includes about 30,000 acres of high-elevation lakes and coniferous forest. It is part of a much larger area under consideration for wilderness classification, extending from the Little North Fork to the headwaters of the North Fork Clearwater River and encompassing 280,000 acres. There are about 280 miles of trails in the entire roadless area with two main entry points from the North Fork Clearwater River. Information on other entry points is available from the North Fork and Avery Ranger District offices.

VIEWING INFORMATION: The most popular trail, along Smith Ridge, is usually snow-free in early July. Mountain goats can often be seen near Larkins Peak and Heart Lake. From the second entry point, Isabella Creek, you can take trails to the Heritage Cedar Grove, a stand of very old western red cedars and western hemlocks. You can also take a trail to Black Mountain, home to a large herd of mountain goats; in July they concentrate around the lookout. Throughout the area you can see elk, deer, moose, and black bear. Forest birds include blue grouse, Clark's nutcracker, gray and Steller's jays, and mountain and chestnut-backed chickadees. A third trail, at the area's southern end, runs for seven miles from one mile downstream of Aquarius Campground to Thrasher Creek. This trail offers a scenic trip through very old stands of cedar and hemlock forest similar to the Heritage Grove. The forest floor is covered with several kinds of ferns making the area shaded and cool.

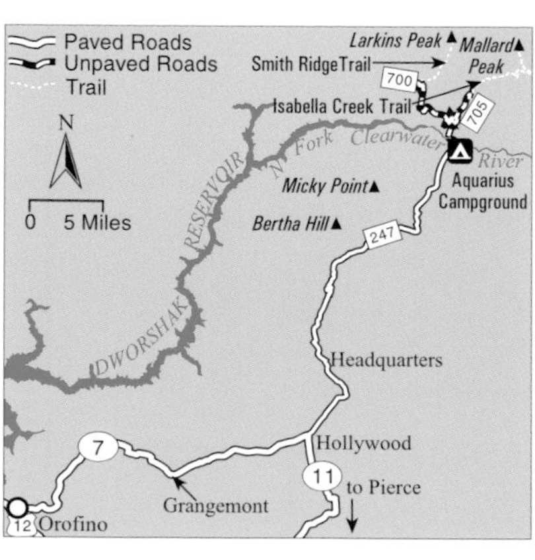

SITE NOTES: Please pick up a Clearwater National Forest map detailing FS roads and trails at the North Fork Ranger office in Orofino.

CONTACT INFORMATION: USFS (208/476-3775, 245-4517)

SIZE: 30,000 acres

CLOSEST TOWN: Pierce

18 HELLS GATE STATE PARK

Common raccoons © George Wuerthner

DESCRIPTION: This is a great birding area just outside Lewiston. The Snake River borders the park in a desert foothill setting. From the campground, there is a two-mile trail that follows the river past basalt cliffs, prickly pear cactus, shrubby riparian vegetation, and grasslands.

VIEWING INFORMATION: Of the park's 121 recorded bird species, Bullock's orioles, eastern and western kingbirds, swallows, and wrens are common, while bald eagles are winter visitors. Among the uncommon species are Vaux's swift, marsh wren, Forster's and common terns, black-crowned night-heron, Lincoln's sparrow, varied thrush, long-eared owl, and common loon. Mammals often spotted include mountain cottontail, white-tailed jackrabbit, and yellow-bellied marmot, while mule deer, river otter, and mink are less common. Area outfitters offer one- and two-day jet boat trips up the river into Hells Canyon (Site #29), the deepest gorge in North America. Park staff will assist you in locating or contacting area outfitters for trip arrangements.

SITE NOTES: Maps and bird checklists are available at the visitor center. The park is open year-round.

CONTACT INFORMATION: IDPR (208/799-5015), ACE

SIZE: 960 acres **CLOSEST TOWN:** Lewiston

19 CRAIG MOUNTAIN WILDLIFE MANAGEMENT AREA

Ruffed grouse © Tom J. Ulrich

DESCRIPTION: This large WMA climbs steeply from 800 feet along the Salmon and Snake Rivers to a one-mile high rolling plateau. This wide elevation range produces diverse habitats supporting excellent wildlife populations.

VIEWING INFORMATION: River flats covered with sand dropseed with scattered hackberry trees attract cedar waxwing and lazuli bunting. The steep bluebunch wheatgrass and Idaho fescue grasslands are home to western meadowlark, vesper sparrow, and gray partridge. Rocky cliffs attract chukar, rock and canyon wrens, falcons, and bighorn sheep. Wet draws and permanent streams with riparian shrubs and trees shelter numerous birds including wild turkey, California and mountain quail, red-eyed vireo, yellow-breasted chat, and several warbler species. The middle and upper elevations give rise to conifer forests favorable to blue and ruffed grouse, Townsend's warbler, ruby-crowned kinglet, woodpeckers, white-tailed and mule deer, and elk. Hunting activities run from September into December. During winter, selected upper plateau roads are open to snowmobiling.

SITE NOTES: See map on page 43. Maps are recommended and available at the IDFG office in Lewiston.

CONTACT INFORMATION: IDFG (208/799-5010), BLM (208/962-3245), PVT, IDL

SIZE: 114,679 acres

CLOSEST TOWN: Lewiston

20 WINCHESTER LAKE STATE PARK

DESCRIPTION: At 4,000 feet elevation, Winchester Lake is at the eastern foot of Craig Mountain, surrounded by conifers and brushy hillsides, with a small marsh at the lake inlet.

VIEWING INFORMATION: Common birds are ruffed grouse, red-breasted and white-breasted nuthatches, common loon, evening grosbeak, Steller's jay, and several waterfowl species. Deer and sometimes elk can be seen in early mornings and evenings from spring through fall. Uncommon species include osprey, turkey vulture, spotted sandpiper, pileated and white-headed woodpeckers, northern flying squirrel, long-tailed weasel, and coyote. Bald eagle, peregrine falcon, and northern goshawk are rare. There is a nature trail next to the park headquarters and other trails around the lake.

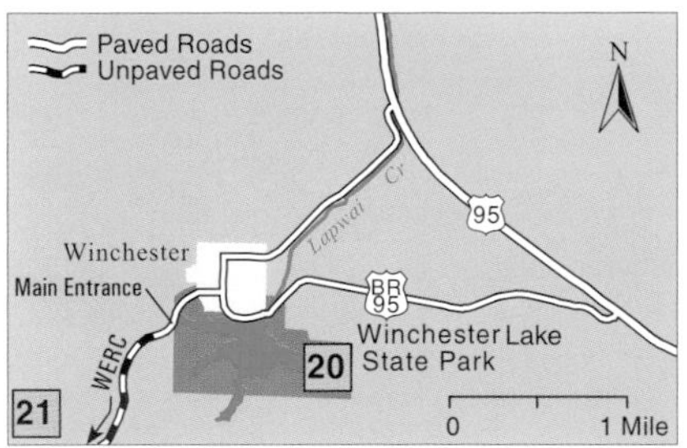

SITE NOTES: Check with park headquarters for information on its interpretive programs and trails.

CONTACT INFORMATION: IDPR (208/924-7563)

SIZE: 420 acres

CLOSEST TOWN: Winchester

21 WOLF EDUCATION AND RESEARCH CENTER

Gray wolf © Jim Dutcher

DESCRIPTION: Located on 300 acres of pristine Nez Perce tribal land, the Center provides a unique opportunity to observe and learn about wolves up close in their natural habitat. The Interpretive Center, an expression of ancient Nez Perce tribal lodges present during the 1805 Lewis and Clark expedition, contains information on monitoring wolf recovery.

VIEWING INFORMATION: Because the wolves are in a 20-acre enclosure, the chances of viewing a wolf are excellent. A trail along a meadow's edge takes you within 50 feet of the enclosure. Guided interpretive walks can be arranged through meadows and forests, where numerous songbirds can be seen.

SITE NOTES: From late May through mid-October, the visitor center and observation deck are open daily. Call ahead to confirm the day's open hours and for guided tour information. Between mid-October and late May, visits are by reservation only. There is a fee for guided tours only.

CONTACT INFORMATION: Nez Perce Tribe, leased and managed by Wolf Education and Research Center (208/924-6960; www.wolfcenter.org)

SIZE: 300 acres

CLOSEST TOWN: Winchester

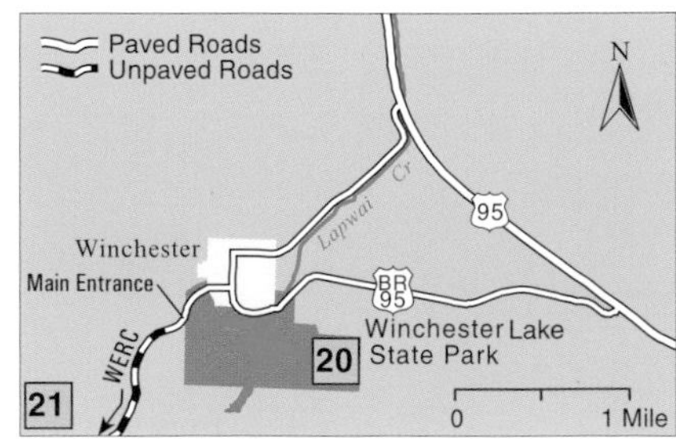

22 NEZ PERCE NATIONAL HISTORICAL PARK — HEART OF THE MONSTER UNIT

DESCRIPTION: As legend has it, the "Heart of the Monster" is a basalt outcropping from which the Nez Perce Indian Tribe was created. It is situated next to the pristine Clearwater River and surrounded by steep mountains covered with pine and fir.

VIEWING INFORMATION: For the best wildlife viewing, follow the paved foot trail beside the river. In spring and summer look along the river for mergansers, Canada goose, osprey, beaver, river otter, mink, and muskrat. Common songbirds include the yellow warbler, Bullock's oriole, western meadowlark, warbling vireo, common yellowthroat, fox sparrow, and spotted towhee. White-tailed deer are often seen at dawn and dusk year-round. Elk may be present in winter as well as bald eagle, tundra swan, and many waterfowl species. This is a popular fall and spring steelhead fishing spot.

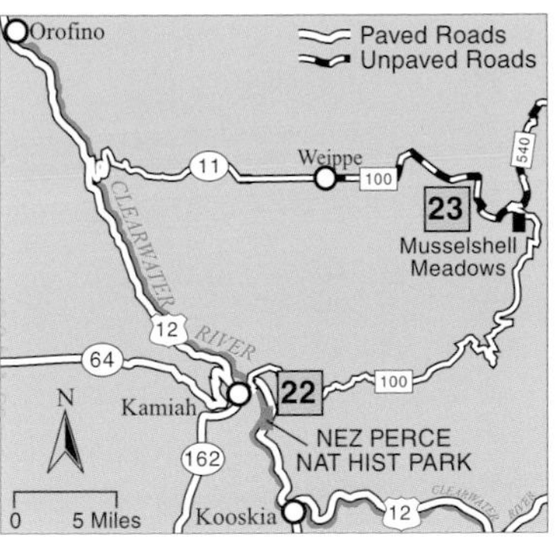

CONTACT INFORMATION: NPS (208/843-2261)

SIZE: 160 acres

CLOSEST TOWN: Kamiah

23 MUSSELSHELL MEADOWS

DESCRIPTION: This site presents a rare mix of marshy meadow habitat within dense coniferous forest. The willow-lined Musselshell Creek flows through boggy meadows and past an old mill pond. The area has a wide diversity of wildlife, especially in spring and summer.

Moose © Leland Howard

VIEWING INFORMATION: Moose with calves, elk, mule and white-tailed deer, otter, woodpeckers, and waterfowl are common. Follow the nature trail; move slowly and quietly to limit wildlife disturbance. Look for warblers and vireos in the willows and phalaropes and American bitterns in waterside vegetation. On early spring mornings, listen for the call of Wilson's snipe and the honks of transitory snow geese. This is one of the few areas in the state that supports fishers inhabiting mature coniferous forests.

SITE NOTES: Road 100 is not maintained during winter. Clearwater National Forest maps are available at USFS stations in Orofino, Kamiah, and Kooskia.

CONTACT INFORMATION: USFS (208/476-4541)

SIZE: 100 acres

CLOSEST TOWN: Weippe, Pierce

24 LOCHSA RIVER CANYON

Calliope hummingbird © Tom J. Ulrich

DESCRIPTION: Part of the National Wild and Scenic River System, this scenic river canyon features steep slopes covered by a mosaic of evergreen trees and deciduous shrubs. The diverse vegetation created by large wildfires in the early and mid-1900's supports one of the nation's largest elk and deer herds.

VIEWING INFORMATION: An excellent place to view moose during summer and fall is at the Elk Summit Cabin south of the Powell Ranger Station. Twenty miles east of Lowell, Wilderness Gateway Campground, near milepost 122, has good birding trails. Common birds include vireos, warblers, hummingbirds, thrushes, and flycatchers. During late spring and early summer, listen to belted kingfisher and Steller's jay calls along the river, where osprey, common merganser, and harlequin ducks nest. In winter look for bald eagles and river otters. The Lochsa River and its tributaries provide important spawning and rearing habitat for steelhead trout and chinook salmon. Trail bridges at mileposts 112, 136, and 152 lead to the south side of the river. A short nature trail at Colgate Licks (milepost 148) interprets on natural resources of the river corridor. Three Rivers Resort restaurant, at Lowell, has several hummingbird feeders attracting black-chinned, calliope, and rufous hummingbirds. The Lolo Pass Visitor Center offers occasional viewing opportunities of moose, elk, and deer. There are good mountain biking trails in the area, and rafting is popular on the Lochsa River.

SITE NOTES: See map on page 50. The Powell Ranger Station is located 65 miles east of Lowell. To reach Elk Summit, turn off U.S. 12 at the Powell Ranger Station sign near milepost 162. Turn left onto Forest Road 111, then take the right fork, Forest Road 360, and continue 12 miles to Elk Summit. USFS maps are available at the Kooskia Ranger Station. Lolo Pass also has maps and information on the area.

CONTACT INFORMATION: USFS (208/926-4275, 942-3113)

SIZE: 65 miles of river **CLOSEST TOWN:** Lowell, Powell

25 SELWAY RIVER CANYON

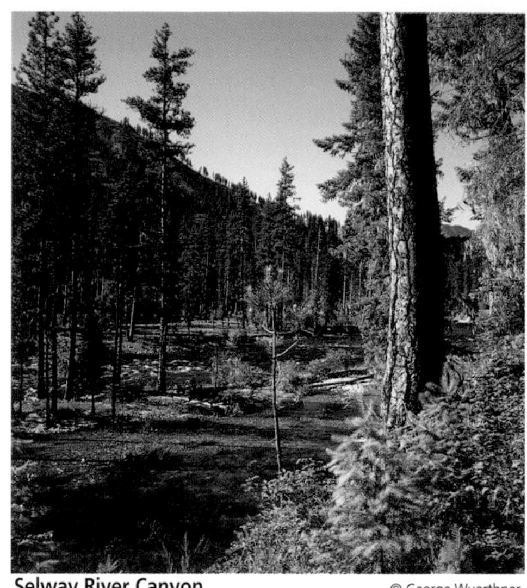
Selway River Canyon © George Wuerthner

DESCRIPTION: The outstanding natural resources of the Selway River corridor earned its designation as a Wild and Scenic Recreation River. The waters are clear and cold, and the corridor is aesthetically exceptional with steep, forested terrain and fern-lined trails. Wildlife is abundant throughout the river corridor. The 1.5-mile O'Hara Interpretive Trail follows the Selway for 0.5 mile then climbs into a cool cedar forest with lush ferns.

VIEWING INFORMATION: Winter and spring are the best times to view elk, moose, black bear, bald and golden eagles, Canada goose, beaver, and river otter. In late spring to fall look for waterfowl (including the rare harlequin duck), osprey, and numerous songbirds. Cedar Flats is widely known as a white-tailed deer fawning area, a great opportunity to see deer in the early morning and evening hours from early to mid-summer. Maintain a good distance from the deer to avoid disturbance. Look for pileated woodpeckers in winter. Recreation opportunities include cross-country skiing at O'Hara and rafting and fishing along the river.

SITE NOTES: O'Hara Interpretive Trail is 6.5 miles from Lowell.

CONTACT INFORMATION: USFS (208/926-4258)

SIZE: 20 miles of river

CLOSEST TOWN: Lowell

   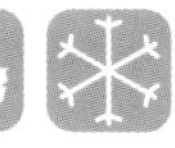

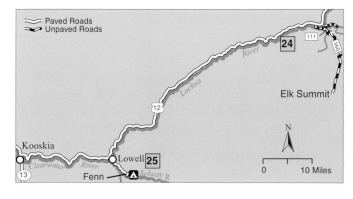

26 ELK CITY AREA / RED RIVER WILDLIFE MANAGEMENT AREA

DESCRIPTION: This area includes the steep, forested canyons of the South Fork Clearwater River drainage and several crystal clear tributaries. Wildlife abounds in this remote and relatively undisturbed area. You will be rewarded by spending time on the area's forest trails.

VIEWING INFORMATION: At McAllister Campground, a 1.25-mile interpretive trail leads to a viewing area where elk, white-tailed deer, and a few bird species can be observed in winter and early spring. Bald eagles winter along the South Fork Clearwater River. At Meadow Creek Campground, a 0.25-mile foot trail leads to waterfalls where migrating steelhead trout jump upstream to traditional spawning grounds from April through May. Newsome Creek and Crooked River are critical spawning and rearing sites for chinook salmon; view them from August to September. You may also see moose, elk, and white-tailed deer in these areas from spring through fall. At the Red River WMA, up to 300 elk have been seen from late April through May in a large mountain meadow. View from your car or the viewing platform to minimize disturbance. Waterfowl, other water birds, and raptors are commonly sighted during spring and fall migration. At Red River Ranger Station, visit the chinook spawning, rearing, and holding facility to see fish up close.

SITE NOTES: There are campgrounds along Crooked and Red Rivers. A Nez Perce National Forest map is recommended for this tour and is available in Grangeville.

CONTACT INFORMATION: BLM (208/962-3245), USFS (208/983-1950) IDFG, PVT

SIZE: 45 miles one-way **CLOSEST TOWN:** Elk City

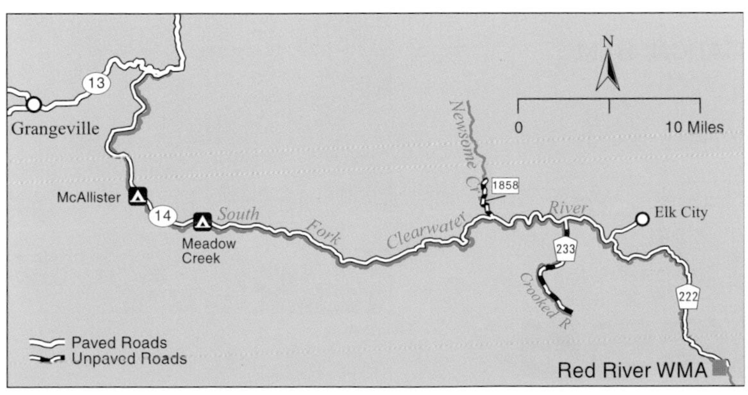

27 LOWER SALMON RIVER CANYON

Lower Salmon River Canyon © William H. Mullins

DESCRIPTION: Bordered by canyon grasslands and steep, rocky cliffs, the Salmon River is the nation's longest undammed river, and the Salmon River Canyon is one of the nation's deepest gorges. The canyon is unique because of its Upper Columbian River Basin flora and fauna. The best way to experience the area is by commercial or self-guided float trip (the latter recommended only for experienced whitewater travelers).

VIEWING INFORMATION: Common wildlife include chukar, golden eagle, prairie falcon, American kestrel, mule and white-tailed deer, elk, and river otter. Although most animals can be seen from the river year-round, the river is not floatable during icy winter months. Hoofed mammals are best seen during winter and spring. Self-guided boaters can launch at Riggins, Lucile, Slate Creek, Twin Bridges, Hammer Creek and Pine Bar. If you view by car, be sure to use turnouts when looking for wildlife. Several commercial guide companies are located in Riggins; they offer half-day to eight-day river trips (contact the Riggins Chamber of Commerce, 208/628-3778).

SITE NOTES: The BLM's guide to the Lower Salmon River is available at their Cottonwood office. BLM registration is requested and is self-issued at the Hammer Creek launch site. Permits and Nez Perce Forest maps are available at the Slate Creek Ranger Station. There are day-use areas at Slate, Skookumchuck, and Hammer Creeks.

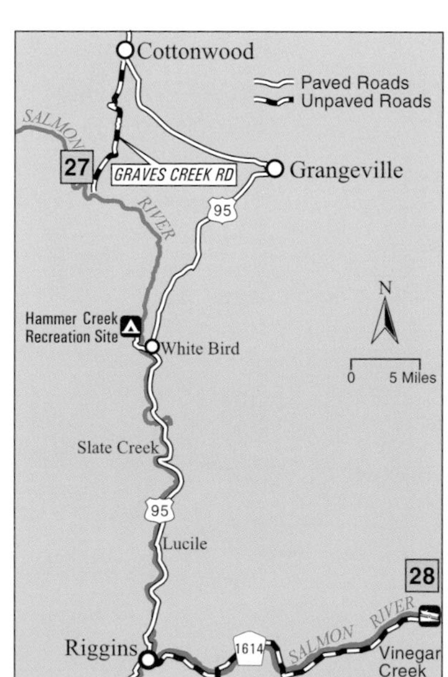

CONTACT INFORMATION: BLM (208/962-3245), PVT

SIZE: 87 miles of river

CLOSEST TOWN: Riggins, White Bird

28 MIDDLE SALMON RIVER CANYON

Mountain lion © Gary Kramer

DESCRIPTION: Called the "River of No Return" by the Shoshoni Indians, the Salmon River roars through the pristine Frank Church River of No Return Wilderness, the largest single wilderness in the lower 48 states. You will travel through a plunging river gorge with magnificent canyon walls and deeply dissected side canyons.

VIEWING INFORMATION: River floaters can often spot small groups of mountain goats and bighorn sheep year-round, but best viewed in spring. Also look for golden eagle, river otter, and waterfowl. The adjoining wilderness area is home to elk, mule and white-tailed deer, moose, black bear, mountain lion, and hundreds of other wildlife species. The numerous hiking trials range from easy to very difficult. Contact the USFS for maps and assistance in planning a backcountry trip. Additional viewing area: The Middle Fork Salmon River, within the Frank Church River of No Return Wilderness, offers 100 miles of outstanding whitewater rafting and good wildlife viewing opportunities. To plan a trip, contact the Middle Fork Ranger District at 208/879-4321.

SITE NOTES: See map on page 52. Several commercial guide companies in Riggins and Salmon offer river trips (contact the Riggins Chamber of Commerce, 208/628-3778, or the Salmon Chamber of Commerce, 208/756-2100). Rafts and kayaks can be launched at any point along the river outside of North Fork. Unguided trips are recommended only for experienced whitewater travelers; permits are required for trips below Corn Creek.

CONTACT INFORMATION: USFS (208/839-2211 Slate Creek, 208/865-2700 North Fork)

SIZE: 80 miles of river

CLOSEST TOWN: Riggins, North Fork

29 SNAKE RIVER IN HELLS CANYON NATIONAL RECREATION AREA

DESCRIPTION: The Snake River, from Hells Canyon Dam to the Oregon/Washington state line, bisects the Hells Canyon Wilderness and travels through the deepest gorge in North America, with rock cliffs up to 5,000 feet tall and gentler grassland slopes. This river section is designated "Wild" from the dam to Pittsburg Landing (31.5 miles) and "Scenic" from the landing to the NRA's northern boundary (36 miles). View wildlife year-round by boat or foot, with best viewing opportunities below Pittsburg Landing. Most people see the area by commercial raft trips; animals generally let you approach closer by boat.

VIEWING INFORMATION: Rugged terrain and isolation provide habitat for many uncommon species including Townsend's big-eared bat, MacFarlane's four-o'clock, and many rare insects. Common species include canyon wren, chukar, elk, mule deer, bighorn sheep, and mountain goat. Occasionally you may see golden eagle and black bear. In winter, bald eagle, elk, mule deer, bighorn sheep, and mountain goat concentrate near the river and may be viewed from the Hells Canyon Visitor Center located below the dam. Stud Creek Trail continues past the Visitor Center, and other foot trails parallel both sides of the river in other places. The Idaho trail runs between Pittsburg Landing and Brush Creek. Be aware of rattlesnakes and poison ivy. Commercial outfitters shuttle people to Hells Canyon Dam from Pine Creek, Oregon, near Oxbow Dam and will also bring them back to Hells Canyon Dam from Pittsburg Landing (a two- to four-day float trip). There are also jet boat tours from the base of the dam, Pittsburg Landing, and Lewiston.

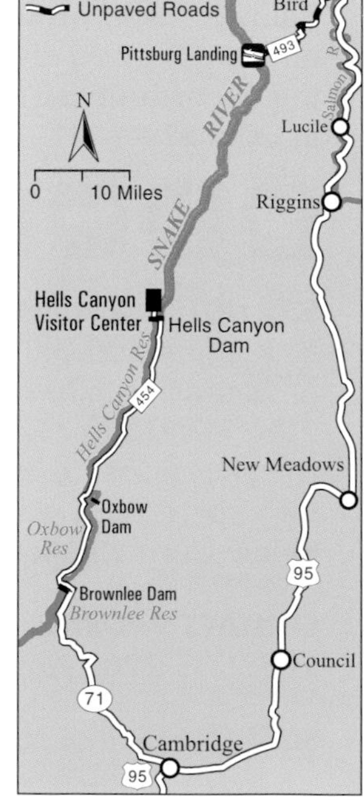

SITE NOTES: Permits are required for all boating from Memorial Day weekend through September 15. Contact the Hells Canyon NRA in Clarkston, WA for a map, backcountry rules, and outfitter information, or the Riggins office (208/628-3916).

CONTACT INFORMATION: USFS (509/758-0616)

SIZE: 67.5 miles of river **CLOSEST TOWN:** Oxbow (Oregon), White Bird

30 SEVEN DEVILS MOUNTAINS IN HELLS CANYON NATIONAL RECREATION AREA

DESCRIPTION: These seven rocky alpine peaks climb skyward from the Snake River to over 9,300 feet and are often snow-capped into July. They provide excellent habitat for mountain goats, best viewed from July to September. Heavens Gate Lookout offers an incredible view of portions of Washington, Oregon, Idaho, and Montana. Several hiking trails lead to over 30 alpine lakes.

VIEWING INFORMATION: Watch for golden eagle, yellow-bellied marmot, Columbian ground squirrel, pika, and the tracks of black bear and coyote. Seven Devils Lake is a popular canoeing spot. There are spectacular meadow wildflower blooms in July with dogtooth violet, trillium, Rocky Mountain iris, and wild hyacinth to name a few. On the drive up, watch for elk, white-tailed deer, and ruffed and blue grouse.

Seven Devils Mountains © Leland Howard

SITE NOTES: See map on page 56. Maps are available at the USFS office, south of Riggins.

CONTACT INFORMATION: USFS (208/628-3916)

SIZE: Over 50 square miles

CLOSEST TOWN: Riggins

31 RAPID RIVER FISH HATCHERY

DESCRIPTION: This fish hatchery is located along the Wild and Scenic Rapid River. The river canyon's steep slopes are covered with open stands of ponderosa pine and Douglas fir, intermixed with stands of mountain mahogany, greenbush, and birch. The hatchery offers a close look at chinook salmon and a lesson on their life cycle.

VIEWING INFORMATION: View adult chinook from May to mid-September, and juveniles year-round. Upstream of the hatchery, a USFS trail bordering the river is a good place to see golden eagle, northern goshawk, chukar, gray partridge, Townsend's solitaire, wrens, and kinglets. The chestnut-backed chickadee has been seen in winter. Watch for western rattlesnakes along the trail, especially in low water years. The hatchery is open all year, seven days a week, with tours available anytime.

CONTACT INFORMATION: Idaho Power Company, managed by IDFG (208/628-3277)

SIZE: Five acres

CLOSEST TOWN: Riggins

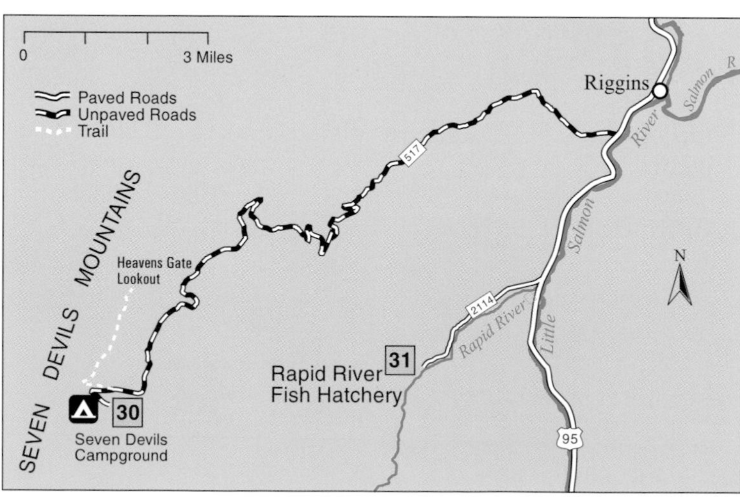

East Fork Owyhee River

© Leland Howard

REGION THREE

SOUTHWEST

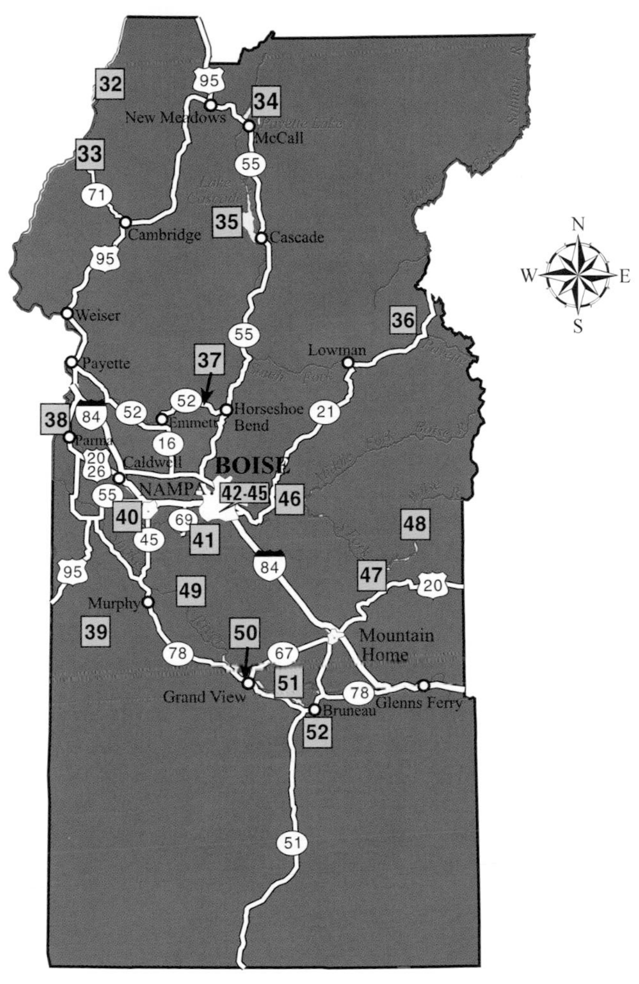

WILDLIFE VIEWING SITES

32 Brownlee, Oxbow, and Hells Canyon Reservoirs
33 Cecil D. Andrus Wildlife Management Area
34 Ponderosa State Park
35 Lake Cascade
36 Bear Valley
37 Montour Wildlife Management and Recreation Area
38 Fort Boise Wildlife Management Area
39 Owyhee Mountains Loop
40 Deer Flat National Wildlife Refuge
41 World Center for Birds of Prey
42 Boise River Greenbelt
43 Barber Park
44 Morrison Knudsen Nature Center
45 Kathryn Albertson Park
46 Boise River Wildlife Management Area
47 South Fork Boise River
48 Upper South Fork Boise River
49 Snake River Birds of Prey National Conservation Area
50 Ted Trueblood Wildlife Area
51 C. J. Strike Wildlife Management Area
52 Bruneau Dunes State Park

32 BROWNLEE, OXBOW, AND HELLS CANYON RESERVOIRS

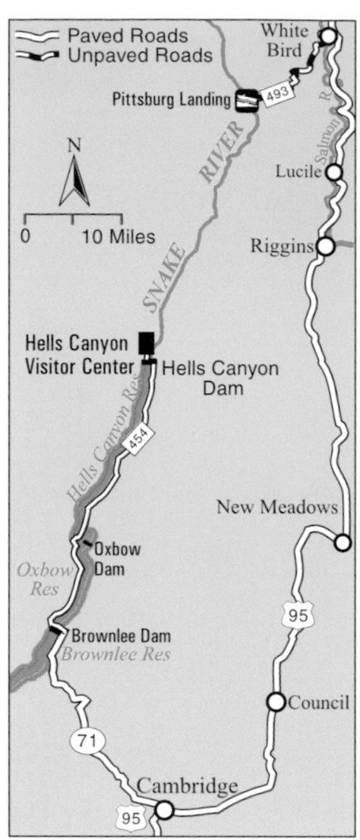

DESCRIPTION: The Snake River flows for 90 miles through three reservoirs before dropping into Hells Canyon, the deepest canyon in North America. Steep slopes covered with bunchgrass, sagebrush, and bitterbrush flank the reservoirs. As you travel north, the terrain becomes steeper with many cliffs scattered with ponderosa pine and Douglas fir trees.

VIEWING INFORMATION: This remote area is an important wintering range for mule deer, elk, and as many as 50 bald eagles on Oxbow Reservoir alone. One can see mountain goats near Hells Canyon Dam and deer and elk along the roadway from December to March. In winter, many waterfowl species use the reservoirs. River otter and upland birds, especially chukar, are common, although not frequently seen. Look for bighorn sheep near Hells Canyon Dam and below Brownlee Dam.

SITE NOTES: Boat access to Brownlee is best from Woodhead Park. At Hells Canyon Dam, a stairway allows foot access to the base and to a trail up Deep Creek.

CONTACT INFORMATION: USFS (208/628-3916), IDFG (208/257-3363), IDL (208/634-7125), BLM, Idaho Power Co. (800/422-3143)

Bighorn sheep © Gary Kramer

SIZE: 90 miles of river/reservoir

CLOSEST TOWN: Cambridge

33 CECIL D. ANDRUS WILDLIFE MANAGEMENT AREA

DESCRIPTION: This WMA abuts the Hells Canyon Complex (Site #32) and has steep mountainous terrain, rolling hills, shrub-covered draws, and about 30 miles of perennial streams. Elevation ranges from 2,000 ft. at Brownlee Reservoir to 5,000 ft. on Cuddy Mountain. Lower elevations are primarily annual grasslands; higher elevations support native fescue, bunchgrass, and sagebrush communities. Douglas fir and ponderosa pine are found at the highest elevations adjacent to the Payette National Forest. iparian areas support cottonwood and shrubs, including hackberry, wild cherry, hawthorn, rose, and alder.

VIEWING INFORMATION: Mule deer and elk are seen year-round but are most visible during winter. Bighorn sheep are found on the rocky bluffs in Duke's Creek. Black bears can be spotted, especially in creek bottoms and on the high elevation slopes, during spring and fall. The WMA supports ruffed and blue grouse, chukar, gray partridge, and California quail. Wild turkeys are frequently near the WMA headquarters. Golden eagle, northern harrier, American kestrel, and other raptors can be seen overhead. Desert wildflowers provide a show of color in spring and host a variety of insects. Rattlesnakes are common, with most other reptiles and amphibians found near creeks and springs. Numerous songbirds inhabit the WMA, including northern flicker, common nighthawk, western meadowlark, lazuli bunting, and hummingbirds. The entire WMA is accessible year-round by hikers, horseback riders, and other non-motorized users. Hunting is popular in fall.

SITE NOTES: An additional viewing area is the Rocking M Easement. Detailed maps are available at the WMA headquarters. Also checkout a key to gain motorized access to gated roads from May through December. Full facilities are available at Idaho Power's Woodhead Campground, adjacent to the WMA along Brownlee Reservoir.

CONTACT INFORMATION: IDL, BLM, PVT, managed by IDFG (208/257-3363)

SIZE: 23,608 acres **CLOSEST TOWN:** Cambridge

34 PONDEROSA STATE PARK

Payette Lake © William H. Mullins

DESCRIPTION: This state park, named for its very old ponderosa pines, sits on a 2.5-mile-long forested peninsula that almost bisects Payette Lake. The park has varied topography and habitats, with arid sagebrush flats, steep basaltic cliffs, dense conifer groves, meadows, and marshes. The park offers nature trails, guided walks with park naturalists, and evening campfire programs. Wildlife diversity is high, though many species can only be seen at dawn or dusk.

VIEWING INFORMATION: During spring and summer look for Pacific tree frog, western toad, long-toed salamander, and garter snake in the two marsh areas, as well as mule deer, grouse, great horned and barred owls, pileated woodpecker, Swainson's thrush, and many other songbirds. Black bear, red fox, badger, and bobcat are rarely seen, although tracks left during nocturnal visits may be spotted. Common winter wildlife include red squirrel, moose, red fox, white-tailed and mule deer, osprey, bald eagle, woodpeckers, and nuthatches. The park is also rich in floral diversity with bright wildflower blooms in spring and summer. Look for lilies, penstemon, spring beauties, trillium, and clematis. For additional viewing, the McCall Fish Hatchery offers viewing of chinook rearing from the egg stage to the pre-smolt stage. Cross-country skiing is popular in the winter. The North Fork Payette River is an excellent wildlife viewing area by canoe.

SITE NOTES: The visitor center has park and trail maps, bird and plant checklists, and wildlife notes. The McCall Hatchery is open year-round.

CONTACT INFORMATION: IDPR (208/634-2164)

SIZE: 1,600 acres **CLOSEST TOWN:** McCall

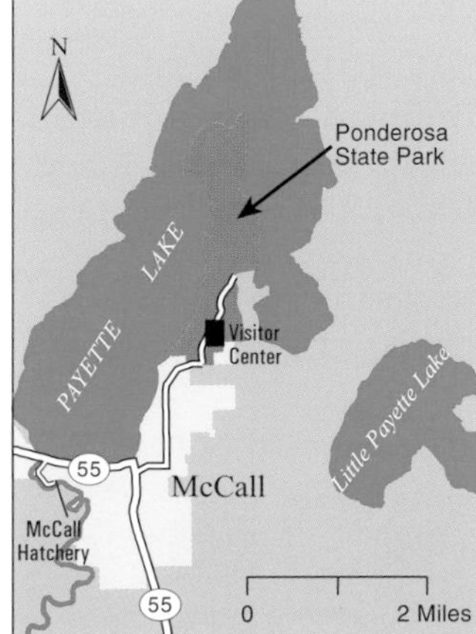

35 LAKE CASCADE

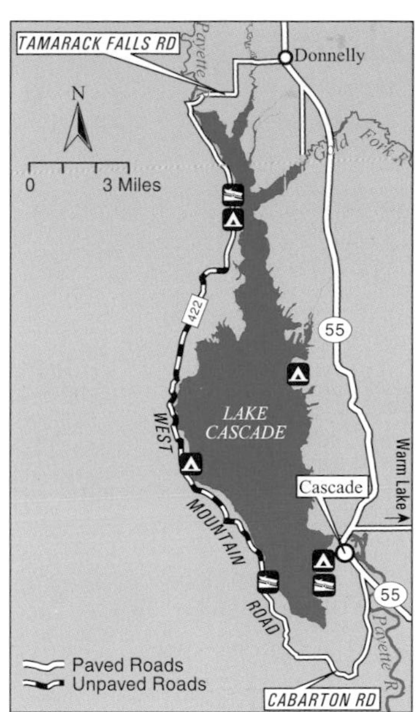

DESCRIPTION: Lake Cascade is rimmed on the east by open fields and on the west by coniferous forest. When the reservoir is full in summer, it is best to observe from the road; when it is drawn down in the spring, fall, and winter, you can walk the shoreline. Mudflats around the reservoir are good for viewing migrating shorebirds and waterfowl. On the east side, numerous small streams and ponds that dot the mudflats provide a vast open area for water birds until the reservoir fills.

VIEWING INFORMATION: Water birds are the main attraction, but avoid all waterfowl nesting areas from Feb 15–July 15. The mouth of Duck Creek is a major nesting area for western and Clark's grebes. Bald eagle and osprey also nest at the reservoir. The calls of common loons are frequently heard. Forested areas are good for viewing Lewis's, downy, hairy, pileated, and black-backed woodpeckers as well as red-naped sapsuckers. Great gray and barred owls have been seen in the lodgepole pine forests; peregrine falcons are seen at the reservoir. Uncommon birds include Vaux's swift, varied thrush, mountain bluebird, Townsend's warbler, American redstart, American pipit, American white pelican, and sandhill crane. For additional viewing, Stolle Meadows on the South Fork Salmon River drainage contains interpretive signs and a boardwalk to view Chinook salmon spawning each August.

SITE NOTES: To reach the salmon viewing areas, go about 20 miles on Warm Lake Rd and cross the South Fork Salmon River. Turn right onto Forest Road 474, and go four miles to Stolle Meadows. You can also view the fish at about 0.5 miles and 15 miles (Poverty Flat) downstream of Warm Lake Road. Maps are available at the Cascade USFS office.

CONTACT INFORMATION: USFS (208/382-4271), USBR (208/382-4258), IDPR (208/382-6544)

SIZE: 28,300 acres of water surface plus 6,000 acres above high water

CLOSEST TOWN: Donnelly, Cascade

36 BEAR VALLEY

DESCRIPTION: This portion of the Boise National Forest is an excellent example of central Idaho's high mountain country, with many mountain meadows surrounded by stands of lodgepole pine and Douglas fir.

Sandhill crane © Tom J. Ulrich

VIEWING INFORMATION: From July to September, in the early morning and evening hours, mule deer and elk leave the timbered forests to feed in the meadows. Observe them from your vehicle. Common bird species include sandhill crane, northern harrier, Swainson's hawk, mountain bluebird, gray jay, and belted kingfisher. Great gray owls, the largest owl in Idaho, have also been observed in the valley. Whitehawk Mountain Fire Lookout provides a wonderful view of Central Idaho. Several waterfowl species can be seen in the ponds at the upper end of Bear Valley Creek. During July and August see spawning salmon in the creek and observe the mountain meadow wildflower blooms. In winter, the tracks of the elusive wolverine have sometimes been seen.

SITE NOTES: There are many hiking trails, and a recommended USFS map is available at the Sawtooth National Recreation Area's Stanley office or the Lowman Ranger Station. There is a rest area at Bruce Meadows. Use high clearance, 4-wheel drive vehicles when roads are muddy or snowy.

CONTACT INFORMATION: USFS (208/259-3361)

SIZE: 16-mile-long valley

CLOSEST TOWN: Lowman

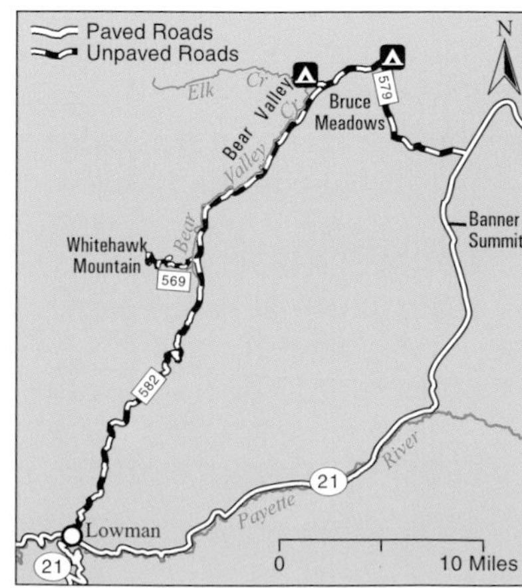

37 MONTOUR WILDLIFE MANAGEMENT AND RECREATION AREA

DESCRIPTION: This area's flooded fields in the Payette River Canyon make excellent habitat for water birds.

Wilson's snipe with young © Tom J. Ulrich

VIEWING INFORMATION: In spring and early summer the area is filled with waterfowl, Canada geese, Wilson's snipe, and blackbirds. Also see osprey, northern harrier, golden eagle, American avocet, Wilson's phalarope, Bullock's oriole, American goldfinch, western tanager, and western kingbird. Look for great blue heron nests downstream of the Payette River bridge and for common yellowthroat and yellow-headed blackbirds in the large cattail marsh on the area's south side. Great horned owls and red-tailed hawks often nest in large trees on the eastern side. In winter, look for mule deer. Portions of the area are closed during the waterfowl nesting season from February to July. For a scenic, easy canoe trip, put in at Horseshoe Bend and take out at Montour Bridge.

CONTACT INFORMATION: USBR (208/382-4258), managed jointly with IDFG (208/465-8465)

SIZE: 1,055 acres **CLOSEST TOWN:** Emmett, Horseshoe Bend

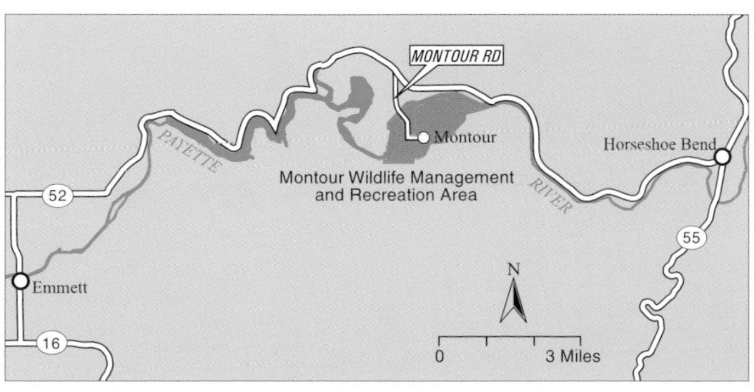

38 FORT BOISE WILDLIFE MANAGEMENT AREA

DESCRIPTION: Fort Boise is at the confluence of the Snake, Boise, and Owyhee Rivers. Cottonwoods and willows line the waterways, with wetlands and artificial impoundments surrounded by cattail, bulrush, and sedges.

VIEWING INFORMATION: Common species include white-tailed deer, turkey, ring-necked pheasant, American avocet, black-necked stilt, black-crowned night-heron, great blue heron, great egret, western screech owl, Swainson's hawk, common yellowthroat, yellow-breasted chat, and yellow-headed blackbird. During winter, bald eagle, merlin, and Cooper's hawk may also be seen. Harris's sparrow, yellow-billed cuckoo, winter wren, pectoral sandpiper, and white-faced ibis are rare. March and April are best for seeing migrating birds, including the greater white-fronted goose. Fishing and hunting are popular.

SITE NOTES: Pick up a map and area guide at the headquarters. Marsh areas are closed during the nesting season, February to July.

CONTACT INFORMATION: IDFG (208/722-5888)

SIZE: 1,500 acres

CLOSEST TOWN: Parma

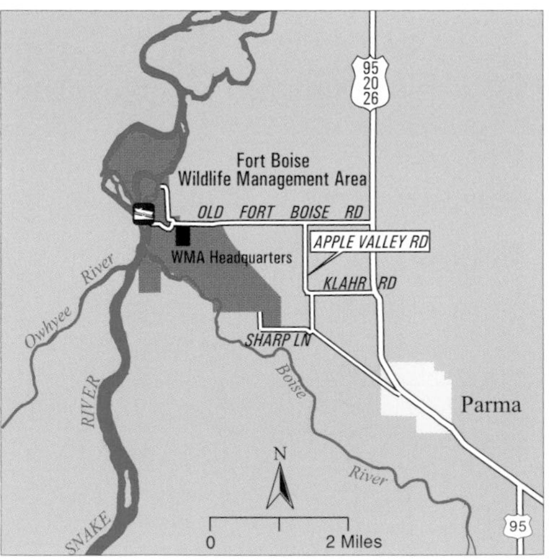

39 OWYHEE MOUNTAINS LOOP

East Fork Owyhee River © Leland Howard

DESCRIPTION: The Owyhees are a rugged and remote desert mountain range in southwestern Idaho. The driving route is generally passable from May to October when roads are dry; high-clearance vehicles are recommended.

VIEWING INFORMATION: From Marsing to Jordan Valley you can occasionally spot pronghorn in the sagebrush grasslands and often will see northern harrier, ferruginous and red-tailed hawks, and golden eagle. Rough-legged hawks are common winter visitors. Near Marsing, watch for ring-necked pheasant, sandhill crane, and white-faced ibis (spring and fall), and mule deer and coyotes in the fields along Jordan Creek. Sage grouse can be observed on their leks (display grounds) in the morning along Glint Creek Rd. and Buchman Grade Rd. from March to May. Endemic redband trout can be seen in perennial streams. Streams also support riparian vegetation critical to desert wildlife including bobcat, red fox, mule deer, river otter, beaver, mink, upland birds, songbirds, amphibians, and reptiles. East of Triangle Junction, stop by Spencer Reservoir to view Canada geese, snow geese, tundra swans, grebes, and various shorebirds in spring and fall. After crossing Toy Pass, several bluebird boxes can be seen north of Hyde Saddle. From Oreana to Walters Ferry you can see a diversity of raptors and occasionally spot long-billed curlews and burrowing owls.

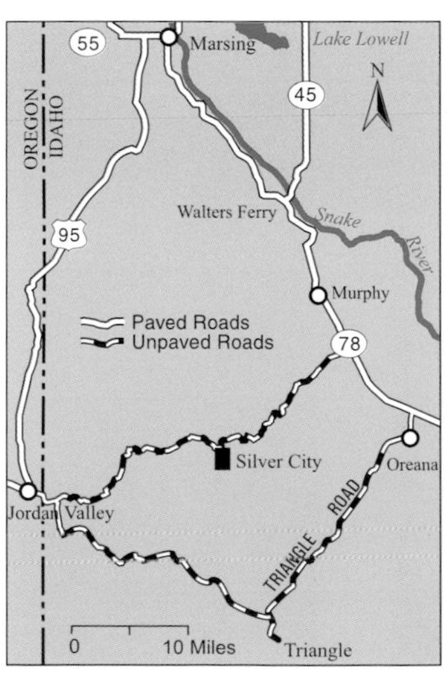

SITE NOTES: From Jordan Valley, turn left on Yturri Blvd., right on Juniper Mountain Rd., left on Flint Creek, and follow signs to Triangle and Oreana. Unpaved roads are not maintained in winter and are often impassable. Total route length is 140-mile round trip from Marsing. Carry drinking water and be sure you have a full tank of gas before embarking on this trip. Camping is permitted on public land.

CONTACT INFORMATION: BLM (208/384-3300), IDL, PVT

SIZE: 140-mile drive **CLOSEST TOWN:** Marsing, Jordan Valley (Oregon), Oreana

40 DEER FLAT NATIONAL WILDLIFE REFUGE

Red-naped sapsucker © Colleen Sweeney

DESCRIPTION: Lake Lowell is a great birding spot with over 200 species recorded. Spectacular bird concentrations occur on the lake during peak migration periods.

VIEWING INFORMATION: Large numbers of shorebirds appear in August when low water levels expose mudflats. Canada goose, mallard, pintail, American wigeon, green-winged teal, and wood duck are numerous from September to December on the lake and in the planted refuge fields. Visiting fall-winter raptors attracted by the abundance of avian prey include bald eagle, northern goshawk, Cooper's, sharp-shinned, and rough-legged hawks, and prairie and peregrine falcons. During April and May watch for migrating songbirds. In spring and summer look for nesting western and Clark's grebes, double-crested cormorant, Caspian tern, sora, Virginia rail, and great horned, northern saw-whet, western screech, long-eared, and barn owls. The 94 migratory bird nesting islands along a 113-mile Snake River sector are best viewed by boat. The islands are closed to public access from February through May. Check in at refuge headquarters for more information.

SITE NOTES: Directions for a car tour are available at the refuge. The lake is closed to boating from October 1 to April 14.

CONTACT INFORMATION: USBR, managed by USFWS (208/467-9278)

SIZE: 11,381 acres

CLOSEST TOWN: Nampa

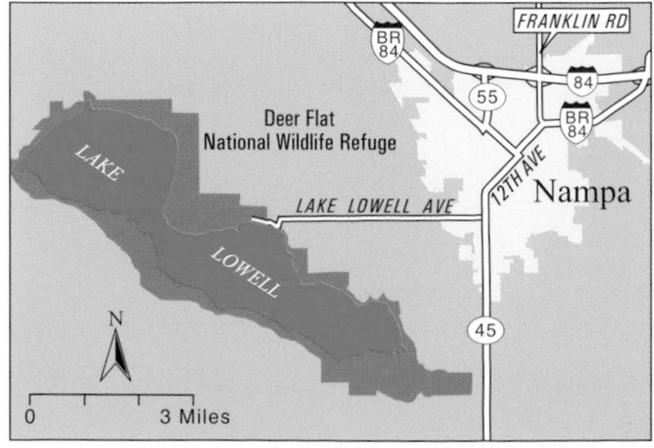

41 WORLD CENTER FOR BIRDS OF PREY

DESCRIPTION: Overlooking southwest Idaho's Treasure Valley, the World Center for Birds of Prey offers visitors an overview of The Peregrine Fund's national and international programs. With projects in over 55 countries, the Center is home to conservation projects for many of the world's rarest birds of prey. After the successful recovery of the peregrine falcon and its removal from the Endangered Species List, the organization continues to successfully breed and release Aplomado falcons and California condors in the United States.

VIEWING INFORMATION: The visitor center gives an intimate view of predatory bird biology, ecology, research, and management. Included are multimedia shows, interactive displays, live bird presentations, a gift shop, and viewing of actual breeding chambers of Aplomado falcons and California condors—one of the few places in the world exhibiting a California condor. On the drive up the hill and from the parking lot, look for chukar, gray partridge, burrowing and short-eared owls, and northern harrier. Open seven days a week.

CONTACT INFORMATION: The Peregrine Fund, Inc. (208/362-8687)

SIZE: 600 acres

CLOSEST TOWN: Boise

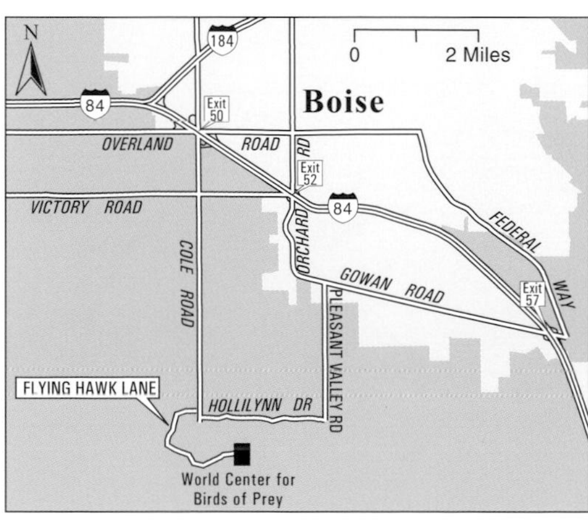

42 BOISE RIVER GREENBELT

DESCRIPTION: The Boise River Greenbelt pathway system links over 850 acres of parks and natural areas with the Boise River's riparian habitat. The Greenbelt provides about 27 miles of paved path and three miles of gravel walking path.

VIEWING INFORMATION: Year-round, visitors can peer through numerous native plant species to view great blue herons, Canada geese, ducks, and songbirds, as well as bald eagles in the winter. Beaver, muskrat, mink, and raccoons are fairly common and usually seen at dawn or dusk. The following three sites are developed wildlife viewing sites adjacent to the greenbelt. Two have unique educational features and the other offers natural viewing.

SITE NOTES: The river is popular for summer floating by innertube, raft, kayak, and canoe. Put in at Barber Park and float six miles to Ann Morrison Park. A map showing the Greenbelt, parks, museums, and other attractions is available from the Boise Park System office (1104 Royal Blvd., Boise).

CONTACT INFORMATION: Boise Parks and Recreation (208/384-4240)

SIZE: 30 miles of pathway

CLOSEST TOWN: Boise

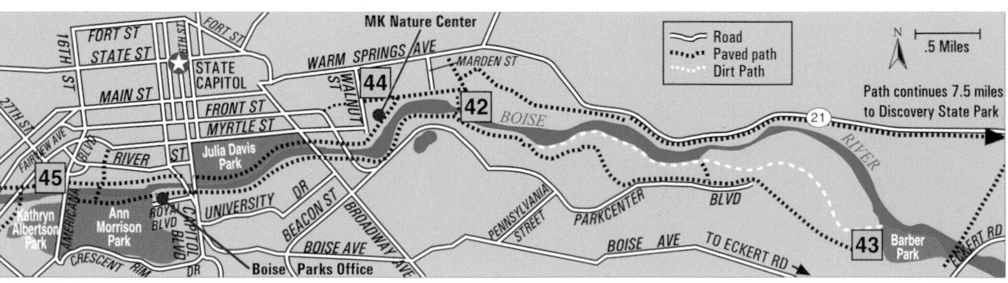

43 BARBER PARK

DESCRIPTION: On the Boise River, this county park offers grass areas for visitors and riparian habitats with cottonwood trees for wildlife.

VIEWING INFORMATION: Bald eagle viewing is from mid-November through mid-March. Perched in large cottonwood trees, adult and immature eagles can often be seen searching for fish. It takes four to five years for bald eagles to develop a white head; younger eagles are mottled white and brown. Stay at least 200 feet from the birds and view with binoculars or spotting scope. Common resident wildlife include great blue heron, Canada goose, wood duck, mallard, California quail, western screech and great horned owls, belted kingfisher, downy woodpecker, northern flicker, mink, muskrat, and red fox. Look along the trail for the telltale tree gnawings of beaver.

SITE NOTES: See map on page 70. The park is located at 4049 S. Eckert Road. The park office is open from Memorial Day weekend through Labor Day weekend. There are inner tube and raft rentals and a launch area.

CONTACT INFORMATION: Ada County Parks and Waterways (208/343-1328)

SIZE: 92 acres

CLOSEST TOWN: Boise

Red fox © David Clark

44 MORRISON KNUDSEN NATURE CENTER

DESCRIPTION: With a river observatory and a wildlife interpretive area, the MK Nature Center is an excellent place to learn about wildlife and fisheries issues and habitat enhancement opportunities.

VIEWING INFORMATION: The observatory is a 550-foot long, cold-water stream replicating an Idaho river. Paths follow its meandering course before dipping below ground level to four underwater viewing stations. Windows reveal the components of an aquatic ecosystem and the life cycle of fish, from incubated eggs to adults. The interpretive area surrounding the stream presents visitors with a cross-section of Idaho outdoors. Also included are a formal backyard setting, rural farm plot, and wildlife viewing windows. Signs give information on wildlife-related topics such as wetlands, snags, and butterfly gardens. You will see bird feeders, nest boxes, and nesting platforms for various bird species. The indoor exhibits change regularly. The Center's goal is to enhance the public's understanding of the value of healthy habitat for wildlife and for people. You can walk through the area or schedule a guided tour.

SITE NOTES: See map on page 73. Nature Center address is 600 South Walnut Street.

CONTACT INFORMATION: IDFG (208/368-6060; messages 208/334-2225)

SIZE: 4.5 acres

CLOSEST TOWN: Boise

Wood duck © Gary Kramer

45 KATHRYN ALBERTSON PARK

DESCRIPTION: This walk-through park was designed as a place for wildlife and visitors alike. A paved path meanders past ponds, trees, shrubs, and open lawn. The park attracts wildlife supported by the adjacent Boise River.

VIEWING INFORMATION: Most conspicuous are waterfowl and songbirds. Waterfowl survival and proliferation is supported by an annual ban on dogs in the park during the nesting season. Two beam and stone gazebos offer attractive views and seating along the paths. Interpretive signs include information on species identification and adaptation, endangered species, and the value of snags, wetlands, and riparian areas. This site also displays a cross-section of the world's largest Ponderosa Pine tree known at the time.

SITE NOTES: The park is located at 1000 Americana Boulevard.

CONTACT INFORMATION: Boise Parks and Recreation (208/384-4240), IDFG

SIZE: 40 acres

CLOSEST TOWN: Boise

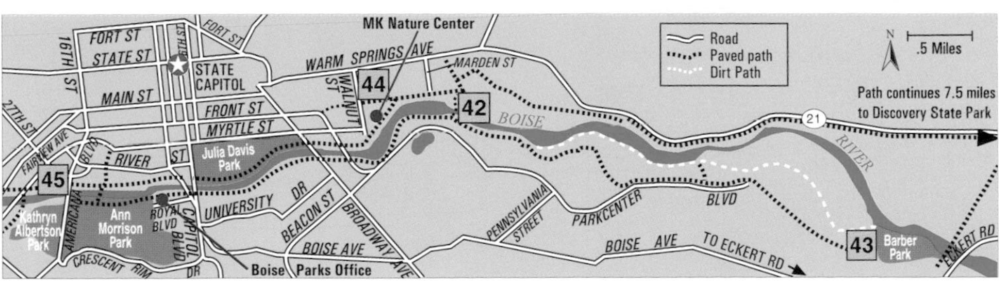

46 BOISE RIVER WILDLIFE MANAGEMENT AREA

DESCRIPTION: The foothills of this WMA are covered with sagebrush-bitterbrush steppe, annual grassland, basalt cliffs, and coniferous forest, providing critical habitat for wildlife, especially wintering mule deer and elk.

VIEWING INFORMATION: Many mule deer and elk winter on the slopes and can be observed from Highway 21 turnouts between December and March. Along the Boise River and Lucky Peak Reservoir look for double-crested cormorants, bald and golden eagles, dippers, and mink. Cliff swallows nest on the cliffs across the highway from the Discovery Park entrance, and rosy-finches use the same area in winter to roost. Highland Valley Rd. transects many habitats and leads up to Lucky Peak, an important migration corridor for birds and location of the Idaho Bird Observatory. A 4WD vehicle is suggested. Two miles past Spring Shores, walk up Mack's Creek and watch for blue grouse, calliope hummingbird, Lewis's woodpecker, yellow-breasted chat, and lazuli bunting.

SITE NOTES: Facilities and boat ramps can be accessed across Lucky Peak Dam at Turner Gulch and at Spring Shores. Use existing turnouts for wildlife viewing.

CONTACT INFORMATION: IDFG (208/334-2115), BLM, ACE, IDL, IDPR, USFS, The Nature Conservancy, PVT

SIZE: 33,540 acres

CLOSEST TOWN: Boise

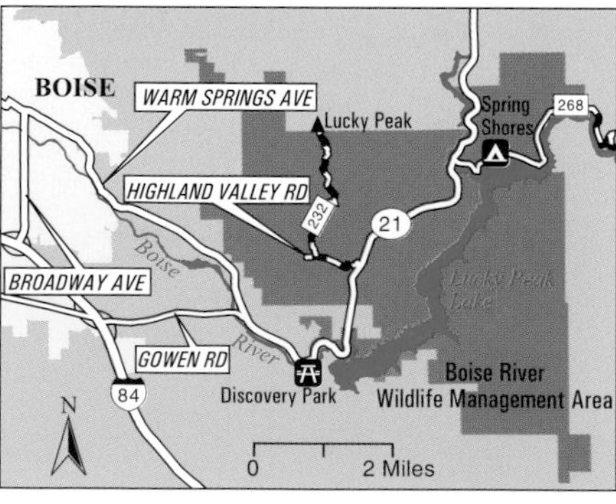

47 SOUTH FORK BOISE RIVER

Lazuli bunting © Colleen Sweeney

DESCRIPTION: A cottonwood-riparian community lines this section of the South Fork Boise River that flows through a steep-sided, relatively open valley. Hillsides are dominated by sagebrush-bitterbrush steppe with a few small mixed conifer stands.

VIEWING INFORMATION: In late summer, turkey vultures float on the canyon breezes around Anderson Ranch Dam. Just below the dam look across the river to one of several osprey nests. The first two miles of the canyon below the dam are narrow, then it opens into a broad valley bottom and the cottonwood-riparian community begins to dominate the river's edge. Look for Lewis's woodpecker, ruffed grouse, Cooper's hawk, great horned owl, warblers, and other songbirds. In the winter, bald eagles perch in the cottonwoods overlooking the river. In the spring, look for spawning rainbow trout. The Cow Creek Bridge is a good place to cross the river and scan the basalt slopes for chukar, golden eagle, red-tailed hawk, and checkout the cliff swallows under the bridge. Other species include beaver, muskrat, weasels, coyote, wild turkey, kingfisher, loggerhead shrike, great blue heron, waterfowl, and shorebirds.

SITE NOTES: Boise National Forest maps are available from the Boise and Mountain Home USFS offices. There are facilities near Pine.

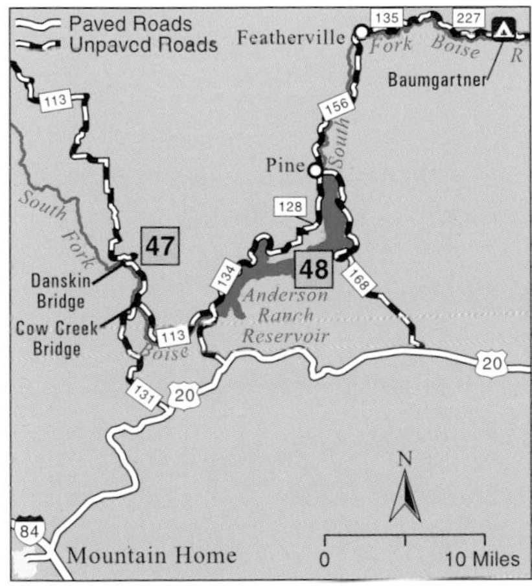

CONTACT INFORMATION: PVT, USFS (208/587-7961)

SIZE: 11 miles of river

CLOSEST TOWN: Boise

 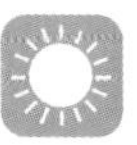  

48 UPPER SOUTH FORK BOISE RIVER

Anderson Ranch Reservoir

DESCRIPTION: The Anderson Ranch Dam, built in 1950, dams the South Fork Boise River creating the 17-mile-long Anderson Ranch Reservoir. Sagebrush plateaus rim the southern end of the reservoir. Ponderosa pines dot the banks of the northern end.

VIEWING INFORMATION: Great blue herons can be spotted near the dam, while bald eagles and osprey nest and hunt along the length of the reservoir. American white pelicans and buffleheads use the reservoir in the fall. Deer and elk winter in lower elevations near the water. Other birds include mountain bluebird, meadowlark, wild turkey, and blue grouse. Golden-mantled ground squirrels and yellow-bellied marmots are commonly seen. In August and September observe kokanee salmon spawning in the river and side creeks. The best viewing is below the bridge at Pine and at Baumgartner Campground. Other native fish in the river include rainbow trout and bull trout. Fishing is a popular activity at the reservoir.

SITE NOTES: See map on page 75. Boise National Forest maps are available from the Boise and Mountain Home USFS offices.

CONTACT INFORMATION: PVT, USFS (208/587-7961)

SIZE: 4,730-acre reservoir **CLOSEST TOWN:** Pine, Mountain Home

49 SNAKE RIVER BIRDS OF PREY NATIONAL CONSERVATION AREA

Snake River Canyon © Larry Ridenhour

DESCRIPTION: The Snake River Birds of Prey National Conservation Area (NCA) was established by Congress in 1993 to protect a unique desert environment that supports North America's densest concentration of nesting birds of prey. Basalt cliffs tower to 600 feet above the Snake River and surrounding lands are dominated by several desert shrub and grass species.

VIEWING INFORMATION: More than 700 pairs of raptors nest each spring along 81 miles of the Snake River Canyon. The ground squirrel and jackrabbit populations provide plenty of food for raptors. Commonly seen raptors include the prairie falcon, golden eagle, red-tailed hawk, and northern harrier. In all, 16 raptor species nest in the area with eight additional species migrating through or wintering. Mid-March to the end of June is the best time to see raptors. Riparian bottomlands provide nesting habitat for lazuli bunting, Say's phoebe, and other songbirds. The NCA has one of the nation's highest densities of badgers and is one of the few places in Idaho to see black-throated sparrows. In all, more than 250 species of mammals, birds, amphibians, fish, and reptiles are found in the area including the Mojave black-collared, leopard, and side-blotched lizards and the night, western ground, and longnose snakes.

Kuna
I-84
KUNA RD
MERIDIAN RD
N
SWAN FALLS RD
Snake River Birds of Prey National Conservation Area
Swan Falls Dam
Map
Area of Interest
0 5 Miles

SITE NOTES: Visitors may tour the area by passenger vehicle or boat. Commercial tours are also available. Maps and brochures on the area are available at the BLM office in Boise (3948 Development Avenue).

CONTACT INFORMATION: BLM (208/384-3300)

SIZE: 485,000 acres **CLOSEST TOWN:** Kuna, Grand View

50 TED TRUEBLOOD WILDLIFE AREA

DESCRIPTION: This area on the north side of the Snake River has three shallow ponds that attract thousands of migratory waterfowl, wading birds, and shorebirds. Islands and heavily vegetated areas adjacent to the ponds provide attractive nesting habitat for Canada geese and several duck species.

VIEWING INFORMATION: Common nesting shorebirds and wading birds include American avocet, black-necked stilt, Wilson's snipe, and killdeer. Yellow-headed and red-winged blackbirds are abundant in the marshy areas while various warblers, sparrows, and other passerines use the dense riparian thickets. Burrowing owl, long-eared owl, and northern harrier are the most common nesting raptors. In winter, watch for ring-necked pheasant, California quail, plus tundra swan and other waterfowl. Golden eagle, great horned owl, and red-tailed, Swainson's, and Cooper's hawks frequently search for prey over the area. Waterfowl hunting is a popular activity.

SITE NOTES: There are three parking areas around the site: one along Idaho 67 and the other two along the river access road that forms the northern boundary.

CONTACT INFORMATION: BLM, managed by IDFG (208/845-2324)

SIZE: 320 acres

CLOSEST TOWN: Grand View

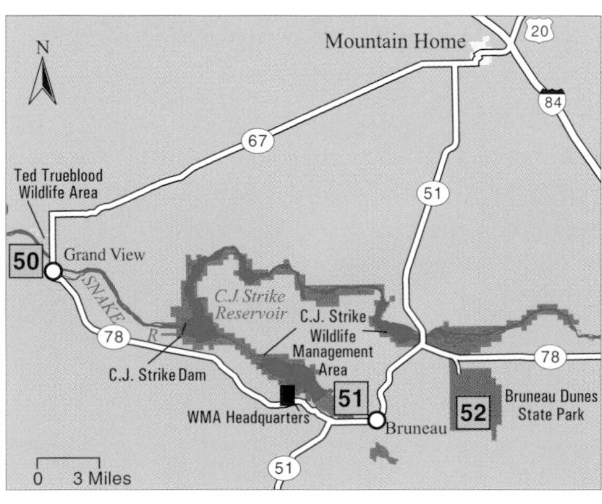

51 C. J. STRIKE WILDLIFE MANAGEMENT AREA

Common garter snake © Colleen Sweeney

DESCRIPTION: This reservoir fed by the Snake and Bruneau Rivers is bordered by marshes, ponds, and wildlife food plots.

VIEWING INFORMATION: Ducks, geese, wading birds, and shorebirds can number in the thousands during migration periods. Many raptor species nest in the area. White-tailed and mule deer are commonly seen at dawn and dusk. Viewers can drive, walk, or bike on many dirt roads that lead to the shoreline, or boat the reservoir.

SITE NOTES: See map on page 78. Pick up a map at the WMA headquarters. This site is a wildlife production, hunting, and fishing area, so there are seasonal access restrictions. Marsh areas are closed from February 1 to July 31.

CONTACT INFORMATION: Idaho Power Co., managed by IDFG (208/845-2324)

SIZE: 13,500 acres

CLOSEST TOWN: Bruneau

52 BRUNEAU DUNES STATE PARK

DESCRIPTION: This state park boasts the tallest single structured sand dune in North America, at 470 feet tall. The dunes are intermixed with sagebrush desert and grassland flats. There are trails around two shallow, marshy lakes lined with riparian shrubs and trees where birds are abundant during migration.

Pheasant tracks at Bruneau Dunes

VIEWING INFORMATION: Most duck species that travel through Idaho can be seen here, and many stay the winter. Water birds include Canada goose, tundra swan, dabbling and diving ducks, and great blue heron. Bald eagles are present in winter. A five-mile hiking trail starts at the visitor center and circles the park, and an excellent interpretive center has wildlife displays. Additional ponds north of the park are good for viewing shorebirds during migration, including the American avocet, black-necked stilt, killdeer, long-billed curlew, red-necked and Wilson's phalaropes, and western and least sandpipers. Look for the resident pair of great horned owls that have nested for many years. The park also abounds with mammals, amphibians, and reptiles, although often only their tracks are seen. Watch for coyote, black-tailed jackrabbit, Ord's kangaroo rat, gopher snake, and short-horned and western whiptail lizards in the early morning or evening hours. Indoor programs are available to schools and other groups at the on-site Eagle Cove Natural Science Center.

SITE NOTES: See map on page 78. Pick up a park guide at the visitor center.

CONTACT INFORMATION: IDPR (208/366-7919)

SIZE: 4,800 acres **CLOSEST TOWN:** Bruneau

   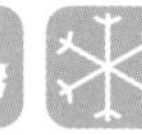        

Snake River at Hagerman Fossil Beds National Monument

REGION FOUR

SOUTH CENTRAL

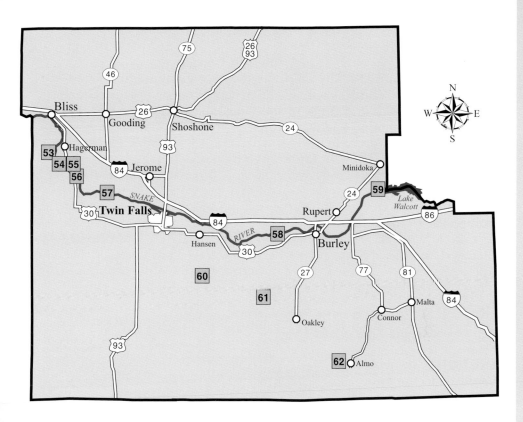

WILDLIFE VIEWING SITES

53 Hagerman Fossil Beds National Monument
54 Hagerman Wildlife Management Area
55 Hagerman National Fish Hatchery
56 Thousand Springs Preserve
57 Niagara Springs Area
58 Milner Lake
59 Minidoka National Wildlife Refuge
60 Rock Creek Canyon/Shoshone Basin
61 Big Cottonwood Wildlife Management Area
62 City of Rocks National Reserve

53 HAGERMAN FOSSIL BEDS NATIONAL MONUMENT

DESCRIPTION: The 600-foot-high bluffs rising above the Snake River and comprising the Hagerman Fossil Beds National Monument are home to Idaho's state fossil, the Hagerman Horse. This site is significant for its variety, quantity, and quality of fossils from 3 to 3.5 million years old. Fossils have been found for more than 140 animal species, both vertebrates and invertebrates, and 35 plant species. No other fossil beds preserve such varied land and aquatic species from the Pliocene Epoch.

VIEWING INFORMATION: The monument offers commanding views of the Snake River and Hagerman Valley and is a good place to view wildlife. Overlooks and trails in the Monument may be accessed from county roads off Highway 30. The Snake River Overlook, at the south end of the Monument, is a wheelchair accessible boardwalk and viewing platform. The Emigrant Trail, which begins across the road from the Snake River Overlook, is a three-mile non-motorized trail. Horse trailers must park at the Oregon Trail Overlook 2.5 miles north. Farther north, a regional trail network offers hiking, horseback riding, and mountain biking opportunities. Do not move or take any fossils, rocks, plants, or animals. If you see a fossil, please do not pick it up; report its location to a park ranger. The visitor center offers close-up views of actual fossils, slide orientation show, and information on how to get to the Monument and trails.

SITE NOTES: The visitor center is located in Hagerman along Hwy 30. Stop by and pick up a brochure and map of the area.

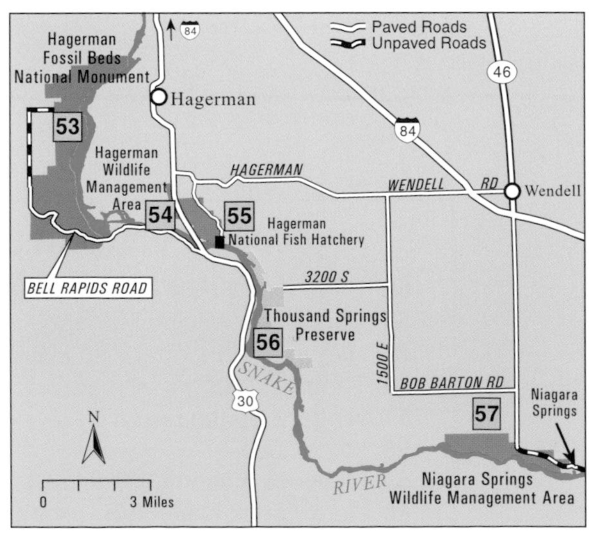

CONTACT INFORMATION: NPS (208/837-4793)

SIZE: 4,280 acres

CLOSEST TOWN: Hagerman

54 HAGERMAN WILDLIFE MANAGEMENT AREA

Snake River at Hagerman WMA © George Wuerthner

DESCRIPTION: U.S. 30 in the Hagerman Valley is known as the "Thousand Springs Scenic Route." Here, the disappearing Lost River of east-central Idaho returns to spew forth a series of white waterfalls down black canyon cliffs. The Snake River Plain aquifer is a massive underground system of lakes and "lost rivers" more than 150 miles long. The clear spring water, at 58° F, is just the right temperature for trout farming. In fact, 90% of the nation's commercial trout is raised in the valley.

VIEWING INFORMATION: Marshy ponds surrounded by emergent aquatic vegetation provide great habitat for waterfowl and wading birds. Common species include Canada goose, mallard, ring-necked duck, lesser scaup, American wigeon, pied-billed and western grebes, American avocet, and black-crowned night-heron. Raptors seen in the area include northern harrier, bald eagle, and great horned and barn owls. Among the less common species are the black-necked stilt, common loon, tundra swan, and Forster's tern. Adjacent uplands are managed for game birds. Fishing and hunting are popular.

SITE NOTES: See map on page 84. Viewing is mainly by driving the roads, but you can also walk the wide, dry dikes from July 15 to October. The state fish hatchery is within the Hagerman WMA.

CONTACT INFORMATION: IDFG (208/324-4359), USFWS (208/837-4896)

SIZE: 880 acres

CLOSEST TOWN: Hagerman

55 HAGERMAN NATIONAL FISH HATCHERY

DESCRIPTION: Located just off the Thousand Springs Scenic Route, this hatchery provides a view of several of the area's well-known springs. These springs are the life blood of this trout- and steelhead-rearing facility.

VIEWING INFORMATION: During late spring, view eggs and fry in both indoor and outdoor rearing units. In summer you can see fingerlings. Sturgeon and a few large trout are located in a viewing pond adjacent to the creek just south of the headquarters. Look for a variety of songbirds in the lush foliage and wetlands that surround the hatchery grounds.

SITE NOTES: Follow signs off Hwy 30. There are interpretive displays, brochures, and a self-guided tour. The hatchery is open year round, seven days a week, 8 a.m.–3:30 p.m.

CONTACT INFORMATION: USFWS (208/837-4896)

SIZE: 300 acres

CLOSEST TOWN: Hagerman

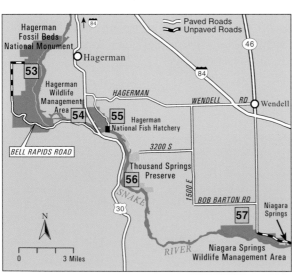

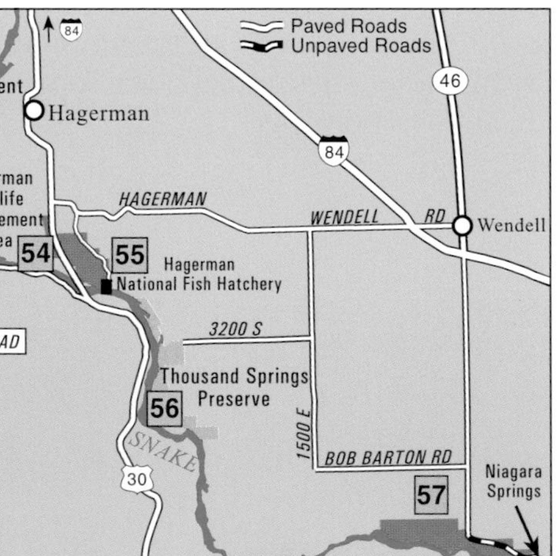

56 THOUSAND SPRINGS PRESERVE

Thousand Springs Preserve © George Wuerthner

DESCRIPTION: This Nature Conservancy preserve includes over two miles of spring-fed creeks and three miles of Snake River frontage, with riparian bottomland and canyon walls up to 400 feet tall. On the preserve's northern end, a spectacular display of springs bursts forth from the fissured, vertical walls of lava rock. This represents the last unaltered canyon wall spring in a system that once stretched for miles along the Snake River. At the southern end are the 400-foot-tall Lemmon Falls and two pristine spring-fed creeks, home to the largest known population of the rare Shoshone sculpin, a bottom-dwelling fish dependent on the spring water.

VIEWING INFORMATION: The preserve is home to over 160 bird species and over 20 butterfly species. Golden eagles and prairie falcons nest on the cliffs, while hundreds of herons nest and feed along the marshes and sloughs. Waterfowl are numerous in winter and migration periods. A good way to see the site and other portions of the Snake River in the Hagerman Valley is by canoe.

SITE NOTES: See map on page 86. At the end of 3200 S, turn left then right onto a dirt road. Park at the Idaho Power Plant Picnic Area, where restrooms are available, and walk across the bridge to the preserve.

CONTACT INFORMATION: The Nature Conservancy (208/536-6797)

SIZE: 425 acres

CLOSEST TOWN: Wendell

   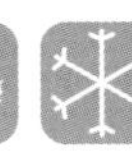      

57 NIAGARA SPRINGS AREA

DESCRIPTION: The Niagara Springs area includes an IDFG Wildlife Management Area, Natural Springs, and Hatchery. The area provides excellent views of whitewater rapids on the Snake River, steep canyon cliffs, and a well-developed riparian ecosystem.

VIEWING INFORMATION: Most viewing opportunities are within the WMA. Common birds seen in spring and summer include the canyon wren, common yellowthroat, yellow warbler, Bullock's oriole, yellow-breasted chat, and Say's phoebe. Waterfowl use the WMA year-round but can blanket the area in winter. Other common species include American white pelican, great blue heron, double-crested cormorant, Caspian tern, golden eagle, mule deer, and various small mammals. East of the WMA is Niagara Springs, a National Natural Landmark where springs bubble and froth as they exit the Snake River aquifer and roar down the canyon wall. Niagara Springs Steelhead Hatchery uses the natural spring water to raise thousands of steelhead each year.

SITE NOTES: Facilities are located at Pugmire Park, on the WMA's eastern side.

CONTACT INFORMATION: IDFG (208/324-4359), IDPR

SIZE: 976 acres

CLOSEST TOWN: Wendell

 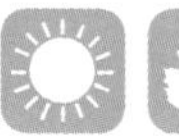  

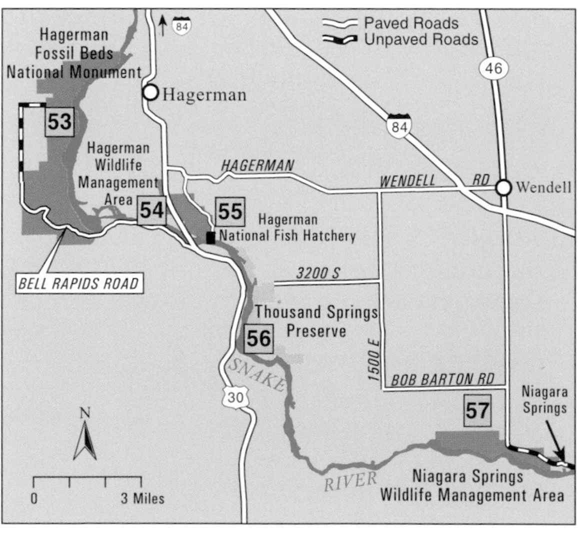

58 MILNER LAKE

Mountain cottontail © Gary Kramer

DESCRIPTION: Milner Lake is surrounded by sagebrush-grassland and lined with basalt cliffs along its northern shoreline.

VIEWING INFORMATION: View water-associated wildlife year-round. See American white pelicans in spring and summer and occasionally bald eagles in winter. Canada geese nest in area juniper trees. Migration periods are best for seeing gadwall, teal, ruddy duck, mallard, and American wigeon. Black-tailed jackrabbit, mountain cottontail, and Townsend's ground squirrel are also common. Mule deer also winter in the area.

SITE NOTES: Turn north off U.S. 30 at the Milner Historic/Recreation Area sign. From the parking area, a sign directs visitors to the boat ramp to the east with additional parking and picnic areas. Walk the shoreline, boat the lake, or travel east on three miles of gravel road.

CONTACT INFORMATION: BLM (208/678-5514)

SIZE: 2,000 acres

CLOSEST TOWN: Burley

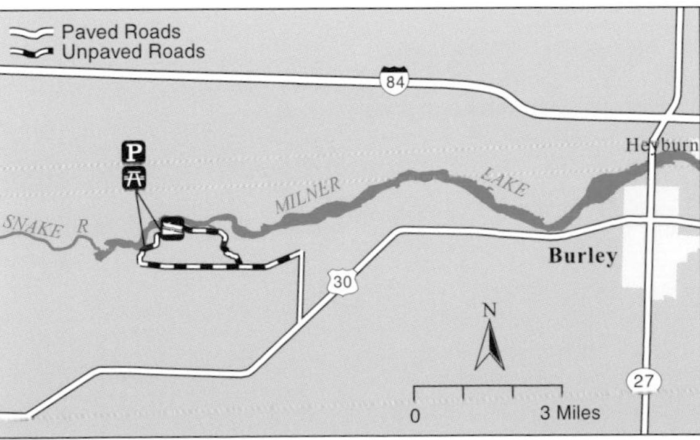

59 MINIDOKA NATIONAL WILDLIFE REFUGE

DESCRIPTION: The NWR extends for 25 miles along the Snake River from Minidoka Dam and includes all of Lake Walcott. The reservoir has several islands and marshy areas. The topography is primarily low, rolling hills and lava rock ledges up to 30 feet high along the shore.

VIEWING INFORMATION: Migratory waterfowl are the most prominent wildlife on the refuge, an important stopover point in the Pacific Flyway. Flocks of over 500 tundra swans, along with 27 other waterfowl species have been recorded.

The refuge has several hundred nesting pairs of American white pelicans. Many songbirds and raptors nest or migrate through the refuge, which also hosts a wide variety of mammals including mule deer, beaver, muskrat, and mountain cottontail. Pronghorn are here in small numbers.

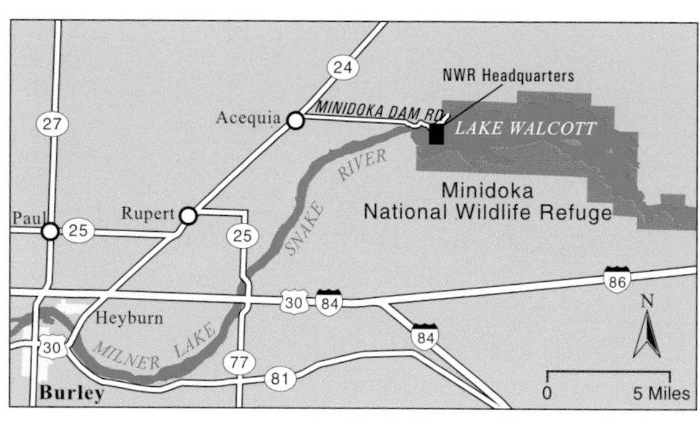

SITE NOTES: Restrooms, picnic area, and campground are located at Lake Walcott State Park. There are three south shore access points for vehicles; sedans are not recommended for the northern access roads. Some roads are closed seasonally to protect wildlife.

CONTACT INFORMATION: USFWS (208/436-3589), IDPR (208/436-1258)

SIZE: 20,699 acres

CLOSEST TOWN: Rupert

   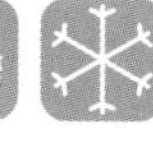

60 ROCK CREEK CANYON / SHOSHONE BASIN

Northern flicker © Tom J. Ulrich

DESCRIPTION: The road through Rock Creek Canyon travels through a steep rock-walled canyon along the riparian-lined Rock Creek. Other areas include a 25-acre marsh (fenced to protect nesting birds) and the Shoshone Basin sagebrush flats.

VIEWING INFORMATION: The canyon offers easy viewing of mule deer on their winter range from December through February. Although winter wildlife viewing is limited, the Magic Mountain area has several cross-country ski trails. Occasionally a porcupine, long-tailed weasel, Steller's jay, or gray jay may be seen. May to October visitors may view wildlife near Electric Spring and in the Shoshone Basin. On the way to these sites, look along Rock Creek for yellow warbler, American goldfinch, belted kingfisher, and northern flicker. At the marsh near Electric Spring watch for island nesting waterfowl and wading birds. Look for the USFS interpretive signs. The Sawtooth Forest has numerous campgrounds and hiking trails. Head west from the marsh into the sagebrush flats of the Shoshone Basin to spot pronghorn and sage grouse.

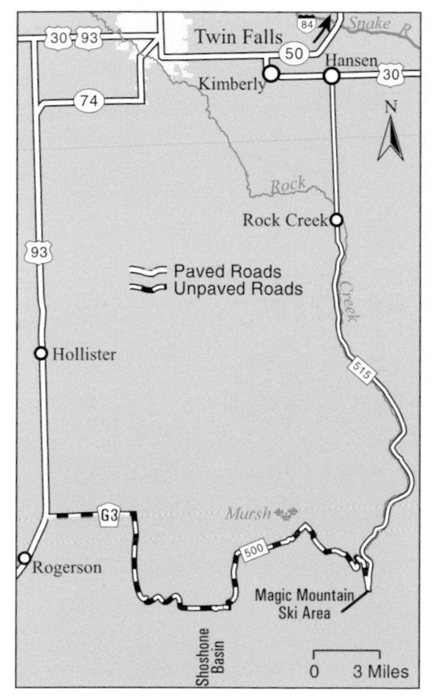

SITE NOTES: Unpaved roads are impassable in the winter. Contact the USFS in Twin Falls for information on ski trails. Maps are available in Twin Falls and Burley.

CONTACT INFORMATION:
BLM (208/678-5514),
USFS (208/737-3200), PVT

SIZE: 40 miles, 5 miles in winter

CLOSEST TOWN: Hansen

61 BIG COTTONWOOD WILDLIFE MANAGEMENT AREA

Western tanager © Tom J. Ulrich

DESCRIPTION: At the mouth of Big Cottonwood Canyon, this WMA lies mostly within the Big Cottonwood Creek flood plain at elevations from 4,600–5,400 feet. Steep talus slopes broken by numerous rock outcrops characterize this canyon area.

VIEWING INFORMATION: The WMA provides a home for a diverse group of seasonal and year-round wildlife. In May and June search the riparian habitats for a variety of songbirds including yellow-breasted chat, lazuli bunting, Bullock's oriole, lark sparrow, and black-headed grosbeak. The rocky canyon and large cottonwoods provide excellent nesting habitat for golden eagle, great horned owl, and Swainson's, red-tailed, and sharp-shinned hawks. American kestrels, northern harriers, and ferruginous hawks annually nest in the sagebrush/juniper uplands and irrigated agricultural lands. In addition, the WMA is a winter stopover for bald eagle, prairie falcon, and Cooper's and rough-legged hawks. Mule deer and wild turkeys are year-round residents. California bighorn sheep frequent the area in late fall and winter. Big Cottonwood Creek supports good numbers of Yellowstone cutthroat trout.

CONTACT INFORMATION: IDFG (208/324-4359 or 862-3479)

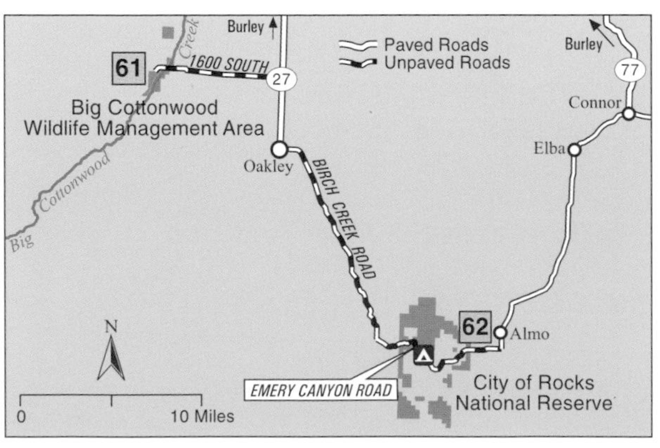

SIZE: 814 acres

CLOSEST TOWN: Oakley

 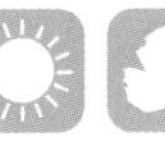 

62 CITY OF ROCKS NATIONAL RESERVE

DESCRIPTION: The City of Rocks gets its name from the grotesque, eroded granite formations of sheer cliffs and pinnacles towering as much as 60 stories above the valley floor. Many emigrants along the California Trail wrote their names in axle grease on these rocks. The dominant vegetation is an extensive stand of pinyon pine, juniper, and mountain mahogany, with occasional aspen and whitebark pine.

City of Rocks National Reserve © Bob Moseley

VIEWING INFORMATION: Songbirds are the predominant attraction, featuring the pinyon jay, western scrub-jay, green-tailed towhee, Virginia's warbler, mountain bluebird, Clark's nutcracker, and Townsend's solitaire. Also find prairie falcon, burrowing owl, poorwill, Say's phoebe, white-throated swift, wrens, common bushtit, gray flycatcher, juniper titmouse, and red-naped sapsucker. This site is world-famous for its challenging rock climbing. Reserve roads are typically closed December through March due to snow.

SITE NOTES: See map on page 92. Camping is permitted in designated sites only.

CONTACT INFORMATION: NPS (208/824-5519), IDPR, PVT

SIZE: 14,400 acres

CLOSEST TOWN: Almo, Oakley

Centennial Mountains

REGION FIVE

SOUTHEAST

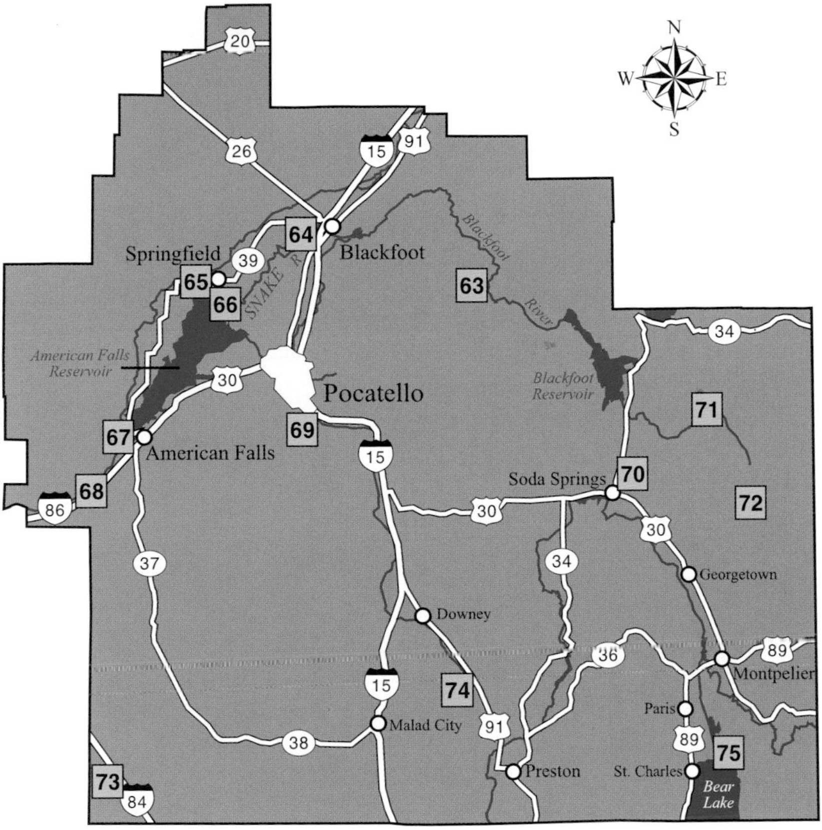

WILDLIFE VIEWING SITES

63 Lower Blackfoot River
64 Snake River at Blackfoot
65 Springfield Reservoir
66 Springfield Bottoms – American Falls Reservoir
67 American Falls Dam and Vicinity
68 Massacre Rocks State Park
69 Cherry Springs Nature Area
70 Formation Springs Preserve
71 Blackfoot River Wildlife Management Area
72 Diamond Creek/Elk Valley Marsh
73 Juniper Rest Area
74 Oxford Slough/Twin Lakes/Swan Lake
75 Bear Lake National Wildlife Refuge

63 LOWER BLACKFOOT RIVER

Lower Blackfoot River © Leland Howard

DESCRIPTION: The Blackfoot River canyon contains steep canyon cliffs and aspen trees providing spectacular scenery and supporting numerous wildlife species.

VIEWING INFORMATION: Cliffs hold nests for raptors including golden eagle, prairie falcon, red-tailed hawk, and great horned owl. Watch for sagebrush inhabitants like sage sparrows, sage grouse, and sharp-tailed grouse along the canyon rim. Songbirds are abundant and diverse with over 100 bird species in spring. Elk, mule deer, and moose are occasionally seen along the river in summer. Viewing for the first 10 miles is from the canyon rim. The next 17 miles have six spots to explore along the river. Rafting is another way to see wildlife.

SITE NOTES: Park in turnouts and walk approximately 200 yards for rim viewing. There are a few road spurs to drive in closer. This route also connects to Grays Lake National Wildlife Refuge (Site #87). A popular rafting run is from Morgan Bridge to Trail Creek Bridge. Facilities are at the campgrounds. BLM land status maps are available at the visitor center in Idaho Falls or the BLM office in Pocatello.

CONTACT INFORMATION: BLM (208/478-6340), PVT

SIZE: 30 miles of river **CLOSEST TOWN:** Blackfoot

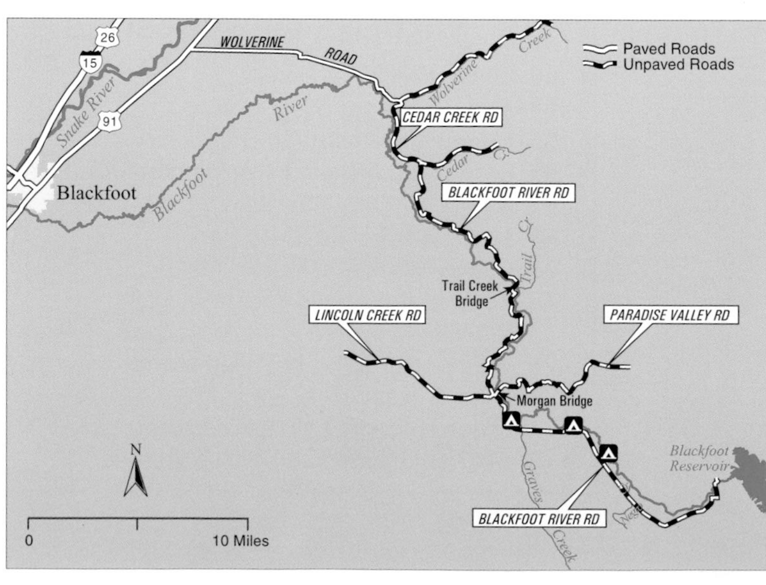

64 SNAKE RIVER AT BLACKFOOT

DESCRIPTION: Below Blackfoot, the Snake River is lined with dense cottonwood stands and flows through agricultural and sagebrush habitats. Most islands and the adjacent cottonwood forest floodplain between Blackfoot and Tilden are public lands.

Great egret 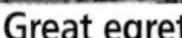 © Gary Kramer

VIEWING INFORMATION: View wildlife by raft or boat from spring to fall. Common species include bald eagle, great blue heron, osprey, Canada goose, mule and white-tailed deer, beaver, river otter, and a few waterfowl and shorebird species. There is a heron rookery along this route, so observers should remain in their craft when near the nests in the spring and early summer. The river freezes in winter and is not floatable.

SITE NOTES: Primitive boat launches are located just upstream from W. Bridge Street. Take out just downstream of Tilden Bridge on the right shore. Check local information on boat ramp and water conditions before your trip.

CONTACT INFORMATION: BLM (208/529-1020), IDL, PVT

SIZE: 10.5 miles of river

CLOSEST TOWN: Blackfoot

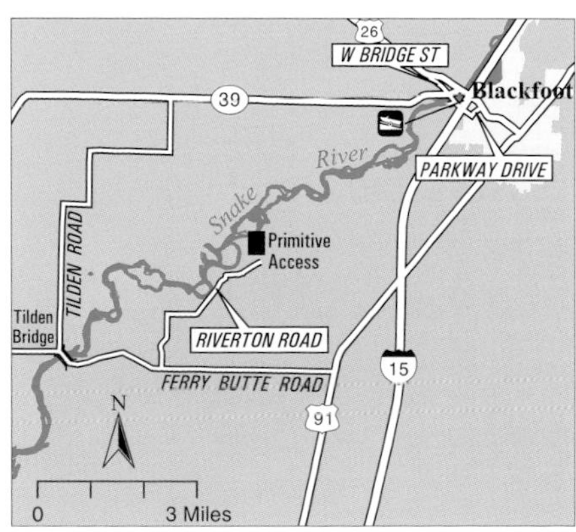

SOUTHEAST REGION

65 SPRINGFIELD RESERVOIR

Northern shoveler © Gary Kramer

DESCRIPTION: Shrubby riparian vegetation and marshland surround this spring-fed reservoir. The Springfield Bird Preserve, mostly private property surrounding the reservoir, is great for bird watching.

VIEWING INFORMATION: Common species seen or heard include tundra swan, common loon, Virginia rail, sora, common yellowthroat, yellow and yellow-rumped warblers, Harris's sparrow, and black-headed grosbeak. Most waterfowl species can be viewed during spring or fall migration. Rare visitors include surf and white-winged scoters, Pacific loon, harlequin, wood and long-tailed duck, greater scaup, and varied thrush.

SITE NOTES: The reservoir is about 0.5 mile west of town. Use road pullouts for viewing. The restroom and picnic facilities are at the city park in Springfield.

CONTACT INFORMATION: City of Springfield (IDFG managed (208/232-4703), PVT

SIZE: 25 acres

CLOSEST TOWN: Springfield

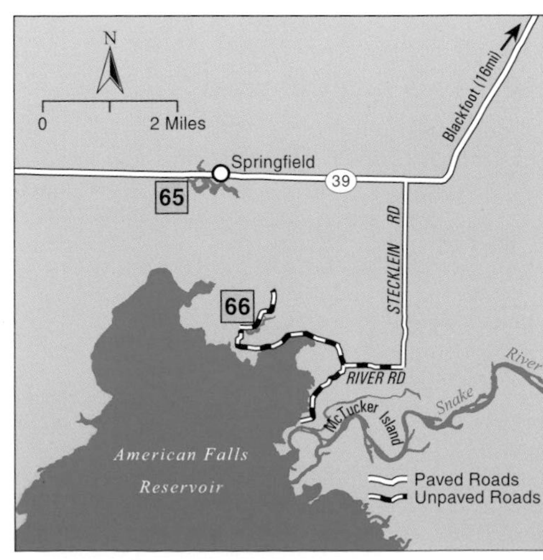

SOUTHEAST REGION

66 SPRINGFIELD BOTTOMS — AMERICAN FALLS RESERVOIR

DESCRIPTION: From mid-July through September these extensive spring-fed mudflats may be the best place in the state to view thousands of shorebirds. Over 8,000 birds representing more than 30 species were counted in one fall.

VIEWING INFORMATION: Abundant species include killdeer, American avocet, long-billed dowitcher, and western and Baird's sandpipers. Some of the uncommon to rare species include greater yellowlegs, willet, whimbrel, ruddy turnstone, red knot, stilt sandpiper, short-billed dowitcher, black-bellied and semipalmated plovers, and lesser golden-plovers. Prairie and peregrine falcons are often present when prey numbers are high. In spring, abundant waterfowl replace the shorebirds. The resident northern saw-whet, western screech, and great horned owls can be found on McTucker Island.

Prairie falcon © Gary Kramer

SITE NOTES: See map on page 98. If the unpaved road is muddy, it is best to stop and walk to the mudflats.

CONTACT INFORMATION: USBR (208/226-2217)

SIZE: Two miles of river.

CLOSEST TOWN: Springfield

67 AMERICAN FALLS DAM AND VICINITY

DESCRIPTION: The ten-mile stretch of the Snake River downstream from American Falls Dam is free flowing river providing habitat for many wildlife species. In winter the entire American Falls Dam area is good for viewing water birds, common loons, and many bald eagles.

VIEWING INFORMATION: Wintering bald eagles communally roost in juniper stands in the Falls View Cemetery; leave that site well before dusk to avoid disturbing incoming birds. Peregrine falcon, parasitic jaeger, and Sabine's and Thayer's gulls are also winter visitors, although rare. During migration over 30 shorebird species have been recorded at the historical American Falls townsite near the silo. In summer, American white pelican, double-crested cormorant, white-faced ibis, terns, and gulls are common.

SITE NOTES: See map showing three viewing sites including 1) Pipeline Recreation Area, 2) Falls View Cemetery, and 3) American Falls Dam. Various Sportman's Access Points provide additional opportunities to reach the Snake River.

CONTACT INFORMATION: USBR (208/226-2217), BLM (208/478-6340), City of American Falls

SIZE: Three miles of river

CLOSEST TOWN: American Falls

   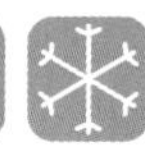      

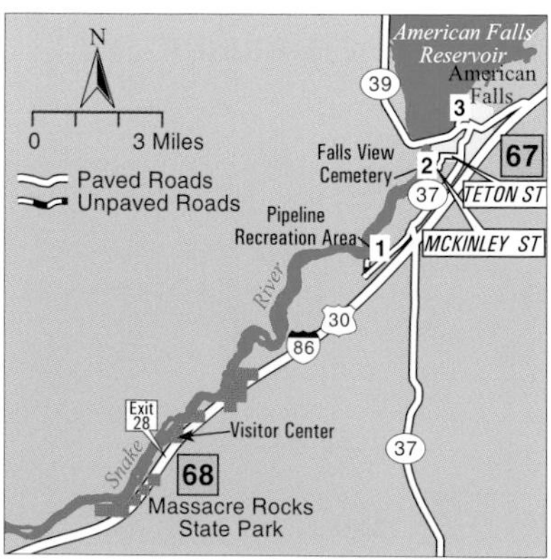

68 MASSACRE ROCKS STATE PARK

DESCRIPTION: This sagebrush desert area, dotted with cindercones, sits adjacent to the Snake River just five miles upstream of the Minidoka NWR (Site #59) and is used by many of the same wildlife species.

VIEWING INFORMATION: Bird watching in spring and fall is excellent. In one year, over 118 different bird species were observed. Mammals are not often seen, although you may spot the tracks or other signs of deer, coyote, badger, bobcat, mountain cottontail, white-tailed jackrabbit, striped skunk, or porcupine. Commonly seen snakes and lizards include the western terrestrial and gopher snakes, sagebrush lizard, and western whiptail.

Snake River at Massacre Rocks State Park © Vitit Kantabutra

SITE NOTES: See map on page 100. Visit the visitor center for trail maps and bird checklists.

CONTACT INFORMATION: IDPR (208/548-2672)

SIZE: 990 acres

CLOSEST TOWN: American Falls

69 CHERRY SPRINGS NATURE AREA

Least chipmunk © Vitit Kantabutra

DESCRIPTION: This site includes three self-guided nature trails with over 50 interpretive signs, two learning centers, and an amphitheater. The trails wind through dense riparian vegetation bordered by mountainous sagebrush-grassland and juniper habitats.

VIEWING INFORMATION: Of the over 100 documented bird species, common nesting species include poorwill, hermit and Swainson's thrushes, black-throated gray and Virginia warblers, green-tailed and spotted towhees, and dusky, gray, and Hammond's flycatchers. During fall and winter, look for the ruby-crowned kinglet, Bohemian and cedar waxwings, warbling vireo, dark-eyed junco, and golden eagle. Thirty mammal and several reptile and amphibian species inhabit the area, although tracks or other signs may be the best way to "see" them. Common mammals include the least chipmunk, red squirrel, white-tailed jackrabbit, western spotted skunk, coyote, and red fox. The sagebrush lizard, western skink, gopher and garter snakes, and western rattlesnake are often seen.

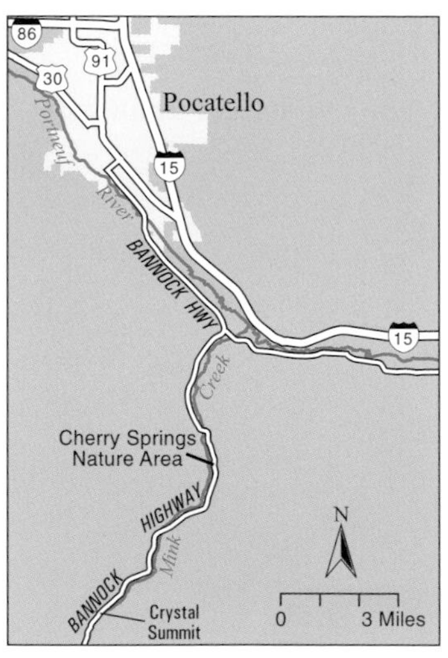

SITE NOTES: Birding is good along Mink Creek and its major tributaries. The Mink Creek drainage begins at Crystal Summit, approximately 4.5 miles south of the Nature Area. Pick up a trail guide and wildlife checklist at the information shelter in the Nature Area. USFS maps are available at the Pocatello Ranger District office.

CONTACT INFORMATION: USFS (208/236-7500)

SIZE: 180 acres

CLOSEST TOWN: Pocatello

70 FORMATION SPRINGS PRESERVE

DESCRIPTION: This preserve protects crystal clear pools and a unique wetland complex at the base of the scenic Aspen Mountains. The cold springs feeding the terraced pools and creek system deposit high concentrations of travertine (calcium carbonate), which gives the site its unique geology. The spring water has been determined to be 13,000 years old. Perhaps the most impressive physical feature is Formation Cave, almost 20 feet tall at the entrance and 1,000 feet long.

Formation Springs Preserve © Vitit Kantabutra

VIEWING INFORMATION: The ponds attract numerous wintering waterfowl. On the preserve look for elk, mule deer, raptors, and numerous songbirds.

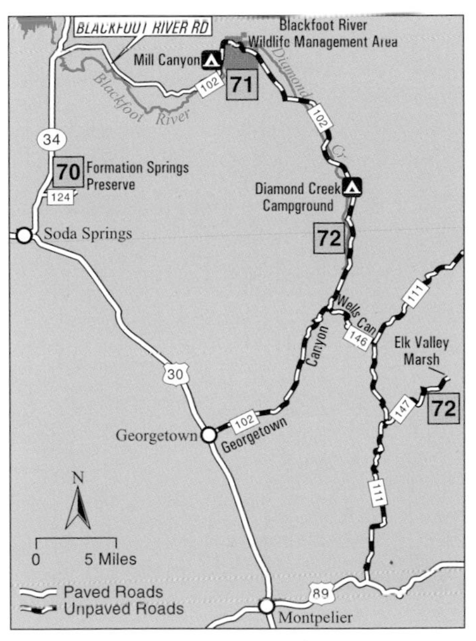

CONTACT INFORMATION: The Nature Conservancy (208/788-8988), BLM

SIZE: 160 acres

CLOSEST TOWN: Soda Springs

71 BLACKFOOT RIVER WILDLIFE MANAGEMENT AREA

DESCRIPTION: Diamond Creek and Lanes Creek converge on this WMA to form the headwaters of the Blackfoot River. Elevation ranges from 6400–7000 feet. Vegetation varies from willow, sedge, and rush communities in the wetlands to sagebrush and aspen interrupted by basalt outcrops.

VIEWING INFORMATION: The Blackfoot River provides key habitat for Yellowstone cutthroat trout. Large spawning fish can be seen in smaller tributaries in early summer. Feeding fish are visible in the main river into late fall. The river, its tributaries, and wetlands provide important breeding habitat for waterfowl and amphibians. Mountain bluebird, savannah and vesper sparrows, yellow warbler, cliff swallow, American kestrel, red-tailed hawk, and ruffed and blue grouse also breed in the area. Bald eagle and trumpeter swan are frequently seen in early spring and late fall. Deer, elk, and moose can be spotted on the slopes or in the meadows in the evening.

CONTACT INFORMATION: IDFG (208/232-4703), IDL, BLM

SIZE: 2,400 acres, 7 miles of river

CLOSEST TOWN: Soda Springs

 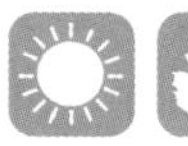 

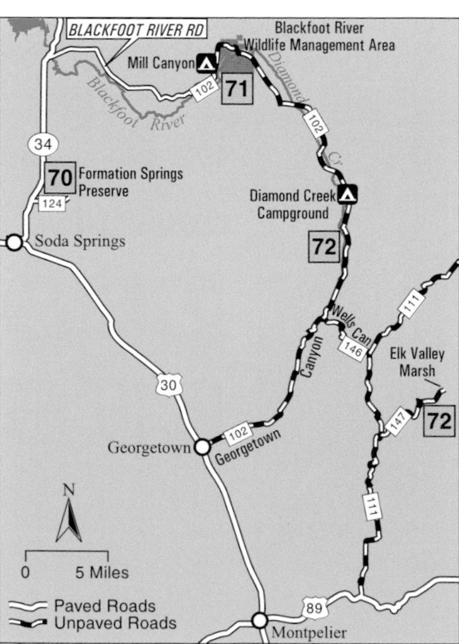

72 DIAMOND CREEK / ELK VALLEY MARSH

Rocky Mountain elk © Gary Kramer

DESCRIPTION: This tour route follows scenic mountain creeks bordered by aspen trees and surrounded by coniferous forest, a good example of eastern Idaho's national forest habitats for wildlife. Elk Valley Marsh is a remote, high-altitude, 200-acre mountain marsh bordered by sagebrush-grassland, conifer forest, and scattered aspen stands.

VIEWING INFORMATION: Beaver dams, which create waterfowl ponds, are numerous, and the state's highest densities of moose are found along Diamond Creek. Willow flats often hide foraging moose in the early morning and evening hours. Also watch for elk and mule deer. Significant numbers of spawning cutthroat trout can be seen from late May to early June in Diamond Creek, where the USFS has installed hundreds of bank support structures, fencing, and pool-creation structures to improve and protect important fish habitat. Elk Valley Marsh is used as a nesting and molting area for Canada geese and dabbling ducks. Sandhill cranes, moose, mule deer, and elk can also be seen. A trailhead starting at Road 147 offers a five-mile loop trail through the Gannet Hills.

SITE NOTES: See map on page 104. Mill Canyon and Diamond Creek Campgrounds have restrooms. There is an undeveloped camping area below Montpelier Reservoir, and two others on Hwy 89 near Montpelier. This tour is almost entirely on gravel roads and is not recommended for cars during wet weather. Many trails can be accessed from this route providing motorized and non-motorized opportunities. A Caribou National Forest map is recommended and can be purchased at USFS offices in Soda Springs and Montpelier.

CONTACT INFORMATION: USFS (208/547-4356 or 208/847-0375)

SIZE: 60–80 mile loop, 20–40 miles one-way

CLOSEST TOWN: Soda Springs, Montpelier

73 JUNIPER REST AREA

DESCRIPTION: This rest area offers easy access in a frequently traveled area for viewing several juniper-associated wildlife species. It is set in the old lake bed of Lake Bonneville.

Ferruginous hawk nestlings © Larry Ridenhour

VIEWING INFORMATION: In winter, look for the juniper titmouse, pinyon jay, western scrub-jay, and rough-legged hawk. In spring, watch for vesper sparrow, mountain bluebird, ferruginous hawk, red-tailed hawk, and northern harrier. View from the parking lot on either side of Interstate 84.

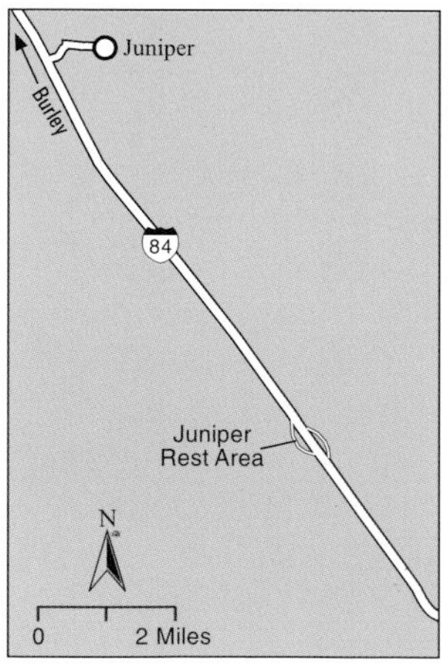

SITE NOTES: The parking lot west of the Interstate is surrounded by BLM land with some unmarked foot paths leading west and south of the rest stop.

CONTACT INFORMATION: BLM (208/766-4766), ITD, PVT

SIZE: 40 acres

CLOSEST TOWN: Juniper

74 OXFORD SLOUGH / TWIN LAKES / SWAN LAKE

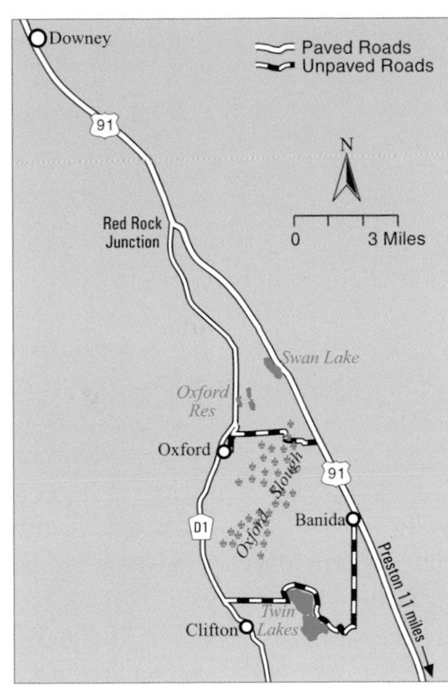

DESCRIPTION: Oxford Slough is a freshwater cattail-bulrush marsh with seasonally flooded alkali flats. Twin Lakes is surrounded by cottonwoods and dry hills, and Swan Lake is a shallow cattail-ringed lake.

VIEWING INFORMATION: Oxford Slough supports colonial nesters including white-faced ibis, eared grebe, snowy egret, black-crowned night-heron, Forster's and black terns. It is also a waterfowl production area, especially for redheads. Trumpeter swans are occasionally observed. Twin Lakes is a staging area for the common loon. Swan Lake is an important spring stopover point for tundra swans and thousands of ducks. Juniper titmice, black-throated gray warblers, blue-gray gnatcatchers, and gray flycatchers can be observed in the surrounding juniper foothills. In winter, rough-legged hawks and northern harriers can be seen throughout.

SITE NOTES: USFS maps are available in Preston, and the Swan Lake General Store has maps of the local area. Land status maps are available at the BLM office in Pocatello.

CONTACT INFORMATION: BLM (208/478-6340), portions administered by USFWS, Franklin County, PVT

SIZE: 5,000 acres

CLOSEST TOWN: Clifton, Oxford

   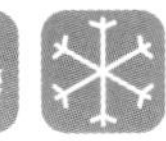

75 BEAR LAKE NATIONAL WILDLIFE REFUGE

Bear Lake © Vitit Kantabutra

DESCRIPTION: This NWR lies in the Bear Valley at elevations from 5,925 feet on the marsh to 6,800 feet on the slopes of Merkley Mountain. It encompasses Dingle Swamp and is comprised mainly of bulrush-cattail marsh, open water, and flooded meadows, which provide nest material, breeding sites, and concealment for small mammals and 165 species of migratory birds.

VIEWING INFORMATION: The Salt Meadow Wildlife Observation Route is a good area to observe birds including waterfowl, avocets, black-necked stilts, and Wilson's phalaropes. The refuge harbors 3,000–5,000 white-faced ibis, one of the West's largest nesting colonies. In summer, western grebe, double-crested cormorant, gadwall, and Franklin's gull are abundant. In September, watch 100-150 sandhill cranes feeding on refuge grains. Winter weather forces most waterfowl south by late November, although you may see common and hooded mergansers, goldeneye, and bald eagle if the water remains open. Mule deer winter by the hundreds along Merkley Mountain and on the Montpelier WMA. One or two moose are present in the refuge willows. Other mammals include muskrat, striped skunk, mink, and mountain cottontail. Five endemic fish species live in Bear Lake.

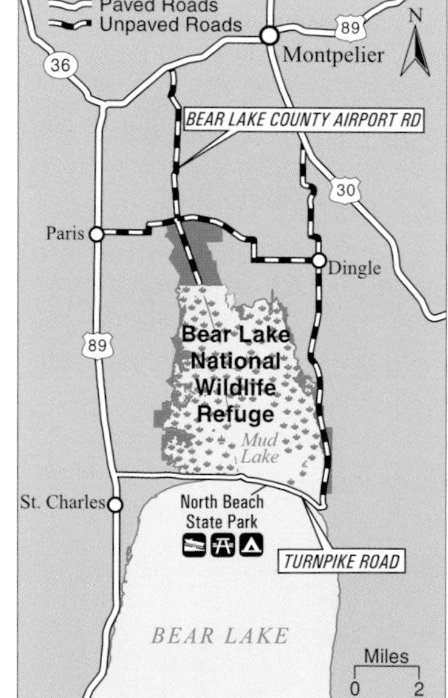

SITE NOTES: Pick up a map and bird checklist on-site or at the headquarters in Montpelier. Restrooms and picnic area are at North Beach State Park. Camping sites are available on nearby USFS lands. Hiking is not permitted from March 1–June 20 to protect nesting birds. Boating is only permitted September 20–January 15. Most interior roads are open to year-round vehicle traffic.

CONTACT INFORMATION: USFWS (208/847-1757)

SIZE: 18,000 acres

CLOSEST TOWN: Montpelier, Paris

South Fork of the Snake River

REGION SIX

EAST

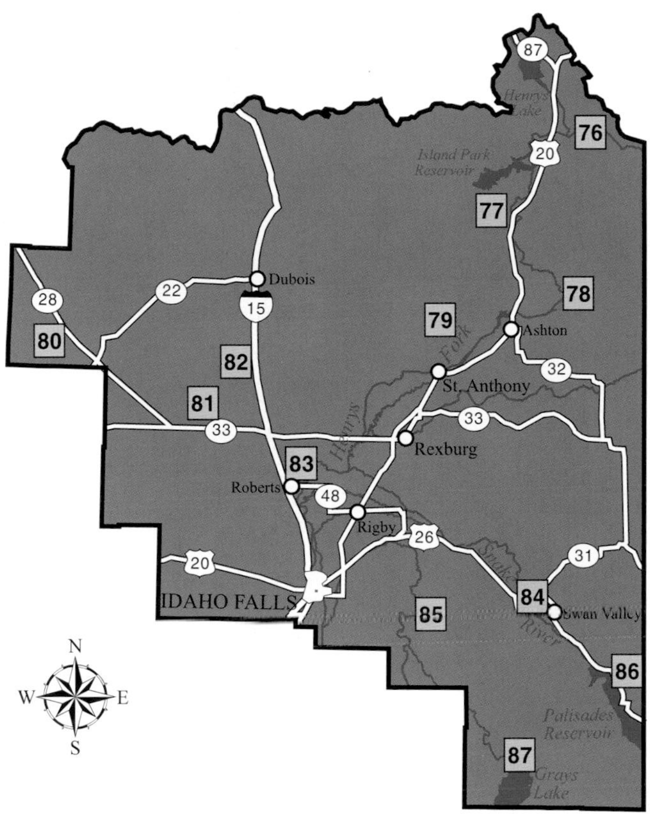

WILDLIFE VIEWING SITES

76 Big Springs
77 Harriman State Park
78 Warm River Fish Observation/Island Park Siding
79 Sand Creek Wildlife Management Area
80 Birch Creek Valley
81 Mud Lake Wildlife Management Area
82 Camas National Wildlife Refuge
83 Market Lake Wildlife Management Area
84 South Fork Snake River
85 Tex Creek Wildlife Management Area
86 Palisades Reservoir
87 Grays Lake National Wildlife Refuge

76 BIG SPRINGS

Great gray owl © Gary Kramer

DESCRIPTION: This site has one of the country's largest springs, producing 120 million gallons of water a day.

VIEWING INFORMATION: Enormous rainbow trout, which feed at Big Springs and are protected from fishing, can be viewed from a 0.5-mile universally accessible interpretive trail. Also look for osprey, bald eagles, waterfowl, and the occasional moose, elk, white-tailed deer, muskrat, and black bear. Use a designated boat launch to travel the water trail by canoe or raft. The trail begins one mile downstream of the springs and offers good wildlife watching during the uncrowded morning and evening hours. Wildlife can be seen year-round, although winter access is limited by snow unless you ski or snowmobile. The surrounding forest contains Idaho's best population of great gray owls. An additional viewing area is Henrys Lake Flat, just north of this site on U.S. 20. This drive-by site is a large, open grassland. In summer and fall, look for pronghorn and sandhill cranes. There are no turnouts in this area, so please drive cautiously.

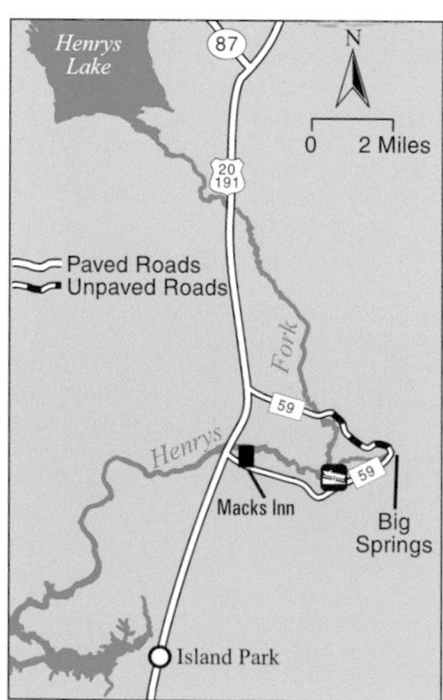

CONTACT INFORMATION: USFS (208/558-7301)

SIZE: Five acres

CLOSEST TOWN: Island Park

77 HARRIMAN STATE PARK

Harriman State Park © Leland Howard

DESCRIPTION: The Henrys Fork of the Snake River courses for eight miles through this park's lodgepole pine forests, meadows, marshes, and two small lakes. The Teton and Centennial (Continental Divide) mountain ranges are visible, as well as the north escarpment of the 20-mile-wide Island Park Caldera.

VIEWING INFORMATION: Breeding pairs of trumpeter swans are the most conspicuous species present year-round. This area is also crucial for up to 3,000 wintering swans from Canada, Wyoming, Montana, and Idaho. Twenty miles of hiking trails pass through meadow, forest, and lake habitats. In open areas and along water courses, look for bald eagle, osprey, Canada goose, many duck species, long-billed curlew, and up to 50 sandhill cranes nesting. In the forested reaches, watch for black-backed woodpecker, Williamson's sapsucker, Steller's and gray jays, red crossbill, western tanager, and the rarely seen great gray owl. Common mammals include elk, mule and white-tailed deer, moose, black bear, beaver, muskrat, river otter, badger, weasel, yellow-bellied marmot, coyote, and fox. Just south of the park, the 30-acre Swan Lake usually has two to six trumpeter swans prior to nesting and a pair with cygnets through September. Moose are also often seen from the turnout.

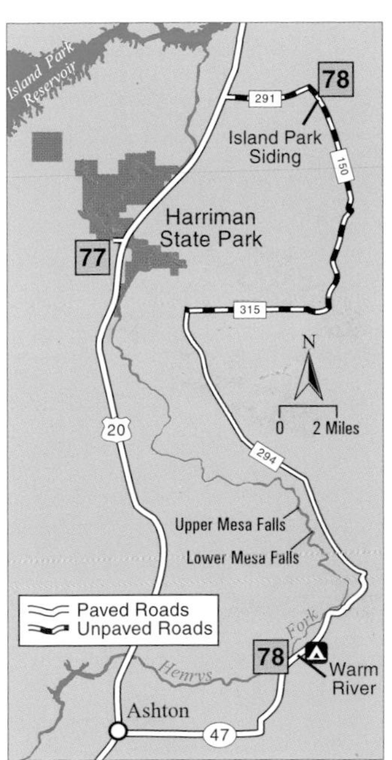

SITE NOTES: Maps and bird checklists are available at the park headquarters. Island Park Dam, eight miles north of the park, also has good bird watching.

CONTACT INFORMATION: IDPR (208/558-7368)

SIZE: 4,700 acres **CLOSEST TOWN:** Island Park

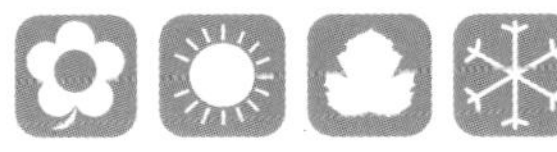

78 WARM RIVER FISH OBSERVATION / ISLAND PARK SIDING

DESCRIPTION: Idaho 47, from Ashton, is a highly scenic mountain drive designated as the Mesa Falls Scenic Byway. There are various turnout areas for viewing. Island Park Siding is a unique one-mile-square area where the forest opens into sagebrush flats.

VIEWING INFORMATION: Look for whitefish and brown, rainbow, brook, and cutthroat trout from a fish observation platform where Idaho 47 crosses Warm River. The best viewing is in summer. Drop a few fish food pellets into the water to bring the fish to the surface. Osprey, bald eagles, and river otter frequent the area. Continuing north, you will pass Upper and Lower Mesa Falls on the Henrys Fork. You can easily see the lower falls from Grandview Campground; to reach the upper falls take Forest Road 295 west. At Island Park Siding, pronghorn feed on the sagebrush and use the coniferous trees for cover. From the road, scan these natural openings for pronghorn in the summer and sandhill cranes in spring and fall. Also watch for moose (in shallow ponds and meadows), elk, and mule deer. There are outstanding wet meadow wildflower displays from mid-May through June.

CONTACT INFORMATION: USFS (208/652-7442, Warm River; 208/558-7301, Island Park), ITD

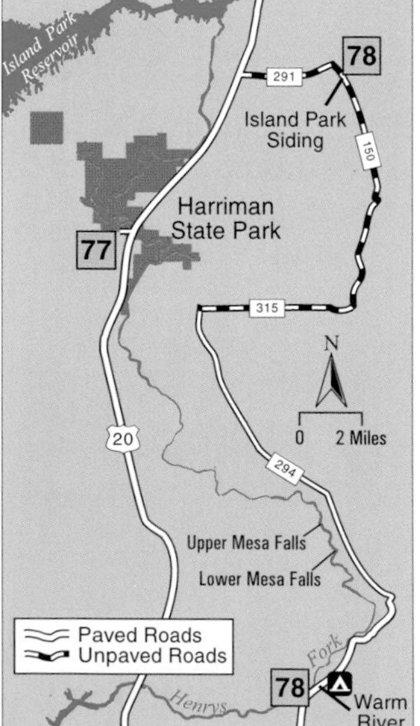

SIZE: 37-mile drive

CLOSEST TOWN: Ashton

EAST REGION

79 SAND CREEK WILDLIFE MANAGEMENT AREA

Trumpeter swan with young © Tom J. Ulrich

DESCRIPTION: The WMA contains a unique blend of diverse geological features including moving sand dunes, lava tubes, broken lava reefs, and cinder buttes. The northern boundary consists of mountain shrub, aspen, Douglas fir, and lodgepole pine habitats, extending southwest into a mostly high desert habitat. The WMA is one of the most important shrub-grass wildlife ranges in eastern Idaho.

VIEWING INFORMATION: The WMA provides many acres of habitat for approximately 170 bird, 38 mammal, six reptile and amphibian, and three fish species at various times of the year. The area provides winter habitat for 3,000 elk, 2,000 deer, and 400 moose. Many wildlife species can be viewed from the major roadways, designated roads and trails, or from the dikes at the Sand Creek Ponds, with the most popular viewing spot at the northern end. In spring, watch for breeding waterfowl and trumpeter swans, sandhill crane, sage, sharp-tailed, blue, and ruffed grouse, golden eagle, osprey, prairie falcon, and a variety of songbirds. Occasionally you can see a bald eagle, common loon, mink, or pronghorn. There are a wide variety and abundance of wildflowers in spring and early summer. Fishing and hunting are popular.

SITE NOTES: Check with the WMA headquarters for breeding and winter closure information. A detailed map and species checklists are available at the WMA headquarters. Primitive campsites are located at Sand Creek Ponds.

CONTACT INFORMATION: IDFG (208/624-7065), BLM, IDL

SIZE: 31,000 acres

CLOSEST TOWN: St. Anthony

80 BIRCH CREEK VALLEY

DESCRIPTION: Birch Creek is a spring-fed stream between the Lemhi and Beaverhead Mountains. This scenic valley is a good place to see pronghorn up close. At the north end of the valley, the Birch Creek Springs Complex is an alkaline spring-seep system merging to form a fertile wetland at the Birch Creek Springs Preserve.
Over the Lemhi Mountains, Summit Creek is another scenic, spring-fed stream.

Birch Creek Valley © George Wuerthner

VIEWING INFORMATION: The Birch Creek Springs Complex supports rare plants, waterfowl, songbirds, raptors, and pronghorn. The rare alkali primrose, hoary willow, and marsh felwort occur in the area. Wildflowers including Kelsey's phlox and shooting stars contribute to a colorful show throughout spring and early summer. Birdwatchers should look for willet, phalarope, long-billed curlew, savannah sparrow, sage thrasher, and ferruginous hawk. There are no established trails, but you can walk throughout the area. A 625-acre area at Summit Creek has well-developed riparian vegetation supporting rare plants and a population of bull trout. In spring and summer, look for yellow warbler, willow flycatcher, American bittern, sage grouse, pronghorn, and rainbow trout. Many species found at Birch Creek also inhabit Summit Creek.

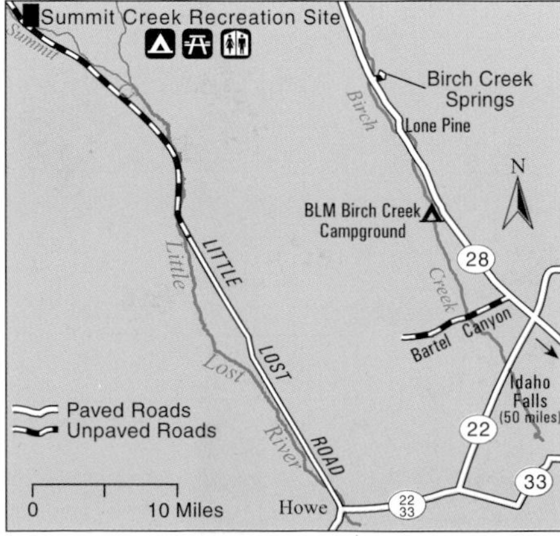

SITE NOTES: Please confine motorized travel to existing roads, and high clearance vehicles are recommended for unpaved roads.

CONTACT INFORMATION: The Nature Conservancy (208/726-3007), BLM (208/756-5400), USFS, IDFG, PVT

SIZE: 2,000+ acres

CLOSEST TOWN: Mud Lake, Leadore

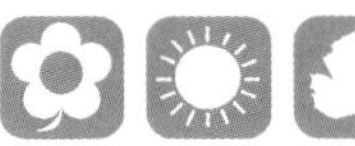

81 MUD LAKE WILDLIFE MANAGEMENT AREA

Pronghorn © Gary Kramer

DESCRIPTION: This shallow lake, averaging five feet deep, is bordered by bulrush-cattail stands, saltgrass, and willows in an area surrounded by tall sagebrush desert, farmland, and pastures. This is an important spring bird migration stopover on the Pacific Flyway.

VIEWING INFORMATION: March to April are excellent times to view large numbers of snow and Canada geese, tundra and trumpeter swans, and many duck species. Other spring birds include American white pelican, Clark's and western grebes, common loon, black-crowned night-heron, white-faced ibis, snowy egret, black tern, and double-crested cormorant. During fall, migrating bird numbers are lower. Shorebird and songbird populations peak in May, and many songbirds stay to nest. Many raptors nest in the area, including red-tailed and Swainson's hawks, American kestrel, and northern harrier. In winter, look for bald eagle, peregrine falcon, and northern goshawk. Mule and white-tailed deer, moose, and pronghorn are present year-round. You can drive, launch small boats, or walk out on several points jutting into the lake. There is a viewing platform near nesting water birds, but from March 1 to July 15 the west portion of the WMA is closed to protect waterfowl breeding. Fishing and hunting are popular at the WMA.

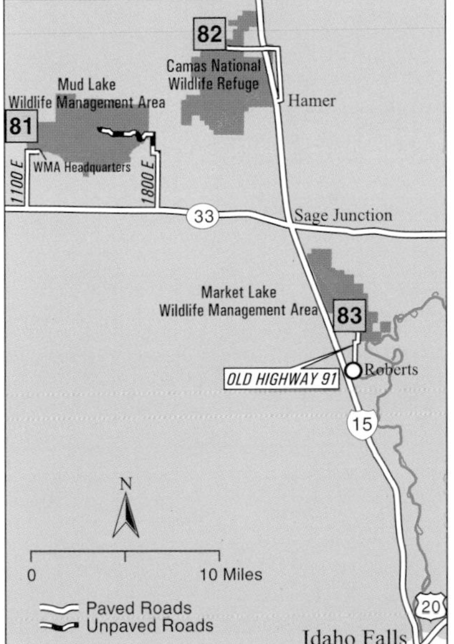

SITE NOTES: Stop at the WMA headquarters for detailed maps and bird checklists. Free camping is for a maximum of 10 days at the north and south boat ramps only.

CONTACT INFORMATION: IDFG (WMA office: 208/663-4664; Idaho Falls office: 208/525-7290)

SIZE: 8,853 acres

CLOSEST TOWN: Terreton

 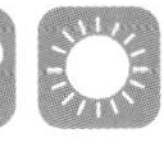  

82 CAMAS NATIONAL WILDLIFE REFUGE

DESCRIPTION: About half of this large refuge consists of lakes, ponds, and marshlands, while the remainder is sagebrush-grass uplands, meadows, and farm fields. Flowing through the refuge for eight miles, Camas Creek supplies water to many of the lakes and ponds. During migrations, up to 50,000 ducks and 3,000 geese use the refuge.

VIEWING INFORMATION: From June to August see large numbers of redhead, mallard, northern shoveler, lesser scaup, and teal ducklings and Canada goose goslings. The rare trumpeter swan also nests here. This is a great place to view raptors, including northern harrier, red-tailed and Swainson's hawks, American kestrel, and great horned, long-eared, and short-eared owls. In winter, observe bald eagles and in summer, look for occasional peregrine falcons, reintroduced on the refuge in 1983. Look also for heron, egret, and ibis colonies. Early summer is an excellent time to view warblers and other songbirds. Scan for shorebirds on mudflats. Frequently sighted mammals include muskrat, beaver, coyote, jackrabbit, deer, and pronghorn. Moose are often seen among willows along Camas Creek.

SITE NOTES: A network of roads on refuge dikes provides exceptional wildlife viewing from your vehicle. A map and bird checklist are available at the headquarters.

CONTACT INFORMATION: USFWS (208/662-5423)

SIZE: 10,578 acres

CLOSEST TOWN: Hamer

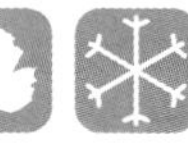

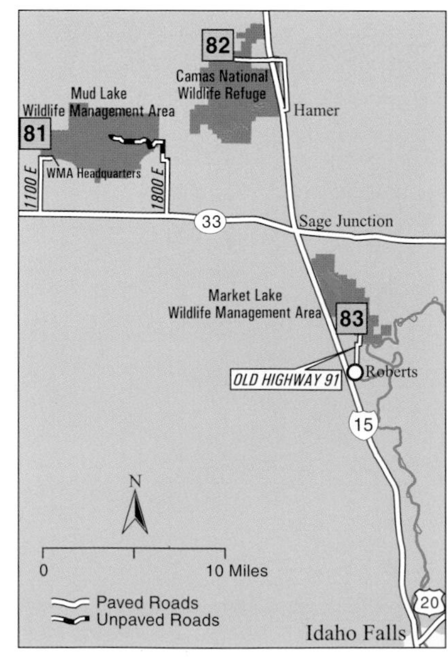

83 MARKET LAKE WILDLIFE MANAGEMENT AREA

DESCRIPTION: Extensive marshes and a canal are surrounded by farmland and elevated areas of sagebrush, grass, and basalt outcrops on this WMA.

VIEWING INFORMATION: Look for large numbers of waterfowl, especially snow geese and northern pintails during spring migration. Other common water birds include tundra swan, white-faced ibis, American avocet, black-necked stilt, black-crowned night-heron, and eared, western, and Clark's grebes. In the emergent marshy vegetation, look for marsh wren, savannah sparrow, and yellow-headed blackbird. Occasionally you can spot a northern saw-whet owl, sora, American bittern, or Caspian tern. Elk winter at the WMA's northern edge. Cartier Slough, situated along the Henrys Fork, has similar species to Market Lake. A mixture of riparian vegetation, marsh, and upland areas provides good habitat for waterfowl, songbirds, and upland birds. Hunting is popular at both sites.

SITE NOTES: See map on page 118. A detailed map and bird checklist are available at the refuge headquarters.

CONTACT INFORMATION: IDFG (208/228-3131)

SIZE: 5,000 acres

CLOSEST TOWN: Roberts

Western grebe © Ken Retallic

84 SOUTH FORK SNAKE RIVER

South Fork of the Snake River © George Wuerthner

DESCRIPTION: The South Fork of the Snake River stretches some 60 miles from Palisades Dam to its confluence with the Henrys Fork. The river flows through narrow channels, around a series of islands, within canyon walls hundreds of feet high, and between farmland flanks. The last 18 miles of river are sheltered by broad, dense cottonwood forest and associated shrubs. There are several boating access sites in the corridor, or you can view from highway turnouts. One spectacular view is the 60-foot Fall Creek waterfall just upstream from the Swan Valley Bridge.

VIEWING INFORMATION: In all, over 80 bird species can be seen along the river corridor, including ducks, Canada goose, great gray owl, peregrine falcon, and the state's largest population of nesting bald eagles. Trumpeter swan, golden and bald eagles, ducks, and geese are present in winter. Also watch for beaver, river otter, muskrat, mule and white-tailed deer, elk, and moose. Never approach heron or eagle nesting or roosting areas; maintain a distance of at least 100 yards while viewing from a vehicle or boat.

SITE NOTES: See map on page 121. A highly recommended boater's guide and BLM and USFS maps are available at the East Idaho Visitor Information Center in Idaho Falls (208/523-1012). The boater's guide shows all boat and river access points, water hazard areas, campgrounds, and travel routes. Check with the Palisades Ranger District for details on road closures and boating restrictions in winter.

CONTACT INFORMATION: BLM (208/524-7500), USFS (208/523-1412), USBR (208/483-4085), The Nature Conservancy, PVT

SIZE: 45 miles of river

CLOSEST TOWN: Swan Valley, Ririe, Rigby

85 TEX CREEK WILDLIFE MANAGEMENT AREA

DESCRIPTION: Diverse vegetation types cover the WMA, including bitterbrush and serviceberry shrub steppe, low sagebrush, aspen, tall sagebrush, Douglas fir, and willow riparian.

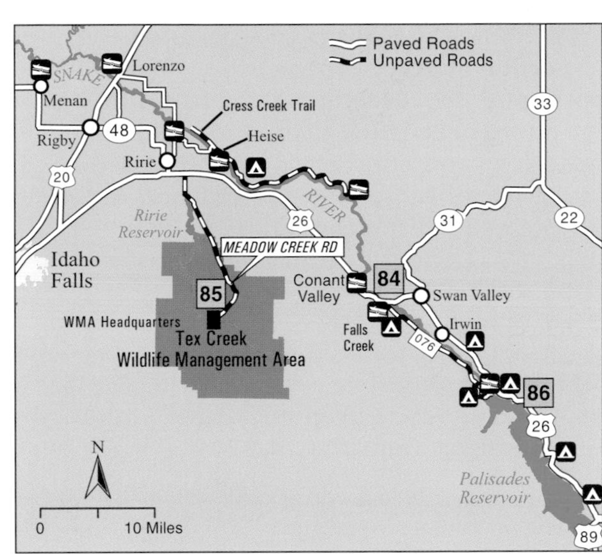

VIEWING INFORMATION: Some 3,000 mule deer, 3,000 elk, and 50 moose are present on the WMA mainly in winter. Other mammals include white-tailed and black-tailed jackrabbits, mountain cottontail, badger, beaver, Columbian ground squirrel, coyote, and red fox. Birds include sharp-tailed and sage grouse, gray partridge, chukar, yellow-rumped warbler, common redpoll, song and vesper sparrows, gray-crowned rosy-finch, cliff swallow, and northern flicker. Common raptors include American kestrel, northern harrier, golden and bald eagles, and northern goshawk. Watch for fall migrating birds including American goldfinch, black-capped chickadee, chipping sparrow, pine and evening grosbeaks, and Bohemian waxwing. Wildflower viewing is popular in spring. The WMA is closed to vehicles December to mid-April and restricted to marked routes other times of the year.

SITE NOTES: All roads are dirt, and a map from the IDFG office in Idaho Falls is highly recommended. Camping is allowed near Ririe Dam and at six primitive sites on the WMA.

CONTACT INFORMATION: IDFG (208/525-7290), USBR, BLM, Rocky Mountain Elk Foundation

SIZE: 31,000 acres

CLOSEST TOWN: Ririe

86 PALISADES RESERVOIR

DESCRIPTION: This high-altitude reservoir surrounded by steep, forested mountains is part of the Greater Yellowstone Ecosystem. It also has a history of a strong nesting bald eagle population.

VIEWING INFORMATION: Look for bald eagle, osprey, western grebe, and great blue heron over the water. Common loons can be viewed in early spring on the reservoir. Along the shoreline at dawn and dusk watch for moose, elk, mule deer, and black bear. The highest number of waterfowl and shorebirds are present during fall, when leaf colors range from bright yellow to crimson red in sharp contrast with the deep greens of the coniferous trees.

SITE NOTES: There are several Forest Service roads and trails to explore. Maps are available at the Idaho Falls Visitor Center or the USFS Ranger District Office.

CONTACT INFORMATION: USFS (208/523-1412), USBR (208/483-4085)

SIZE: 17,000 acres

CLOSEST TOWN: Swan Valley

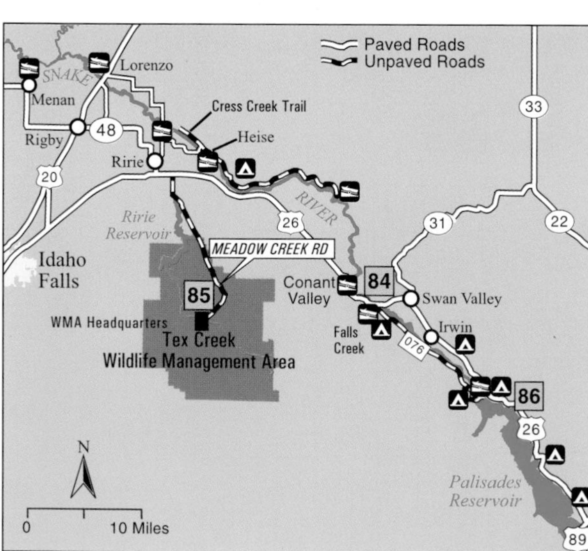

87 GRAYS LAKE NATIONAL WILDLIFE REFUGE

Grays Lake National Wildlife Refuge
© George Wuerthner

DESCRIPTION: This "lake" is actually a large, shallow marsh with dense bulrush-cattail vegetation and very little open water. The refuge is home to the world's largest breeding concentration of greater sandhill cranes.

VIEWING INFORMATION: In late September to early October, up to 3,000 sandhill cranes gather before migrating to New Mexico, Arizona, and Mexico. May and June are the best months to see a variety of wildlife. The marsh is a major producer of Canada geese and many species of diving and dabbling ducks. Franklin's gulls nest in large colonies of up to 40,000 birds. Grebes, bitterns, and elusive rails nest in bulrush. Wet meadows, shallow water, and mudflats harbor curlews, snipes, willets, and phalaropes. Rare bird sightings include lark bunting, bobolink, and peregrine falcon. Common mammals include muskrat, badger, and moose. The roads encircling the refuge offer some viewing opportunities but are impassable in winter. Hiking and cross-country skiing is allowed from October 10 through March 31, but only in the northern half of the refuge.

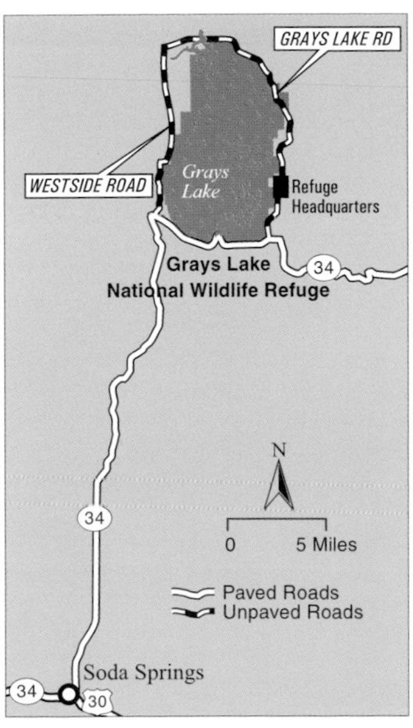

SITE NOTES: The refuge headquarters and visitor center has maps, wildlife checklists, an interpretive exhibit, and observation platform.

CONTACT INFORMATION: USFWS (208/574-2755), BLM, IDL, PVT

SIZE: 18,300 acres

CLOSEST TOWN: Soda Springs

Sawtooth Valley

REGION SEVEN

CENTRAL

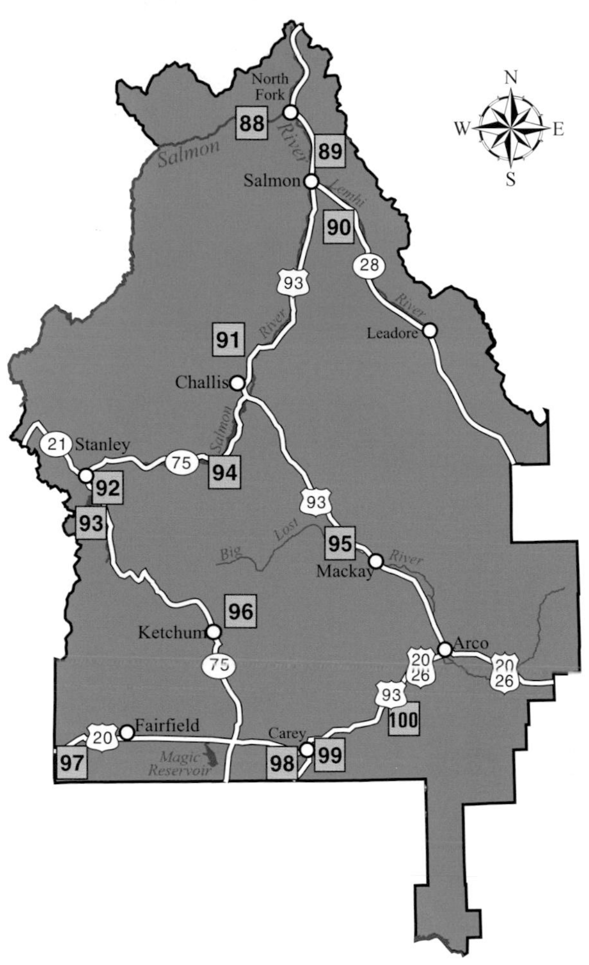

WILDLIFE VIEWING SITES

88 Main Salmon River – Deadwater Slough
89 Upper Salmon River – Salmon to North Fork
90 Lemhi River – Salmon to Leadore
91 Morgan Creek
92 Sawtooth Fish Hatchery/Indian Riffles
93 Redfish Lake/Sawtooth Valley
94 East Fork Salmon River Canyon
95 Mackay Reservoir/Chilly Slough
96 Trail Creek/Corral Creek
97 Camas Prairie Centennial Marsh
98 Silver Creek Preserve
99 Carey Lake Wildlife Management Area
100 Craters of the Moon National Monument

88 MAIN SALMON RIVER — DEADWATER SLOUGH

Main Salmon River © George Wuerthner

DESCRIPTION: Deadwater Slough is a nearly 3-mile complex of two large grassy meadows, braided stream channels, islands, and shallow backwater sloughs along the Salmon River. Shrubby vegetation and cottonwoods line the river floodplain while steep canyon slopes covered with Douglas fir and sagebrush rise above the river.

VIEWING INFORMATION: Deadwater Slough and nearby uplands are excellent birding areas. During summer and fall, hiking, rafting, and kayaking are great ways to view wildlife. Common birds include Lewis's woodpecker, MacGillivray's warbler, Clark's nutcracker, canyon wren, gray catbird, and lazuli bunting. The Salmon River Canyon from North Fork to Corn Creek (46.4 miles) is excellent for viewing bald eagle, beaver, river otter, mule deer, elk, bighorn sheep, mountain goat, and rarely mountain lion, bobcat, and wolf. Two pictograph sites can be viewed near Pine Creek and at Ebenezer. Several rugged hiking trails (Owl Creek, Sheepeater, and Stoddard Pack Trails) can be accessed along FR 30. Slightly easier hiking starts at Corn Creek to either Horse Creek (4 miles) or Lantz Bar (10 miles). Corn Creek is the launch site for Middle Salmon River float trips (Site #28). Watch for rattlesnakes during summer and fall.

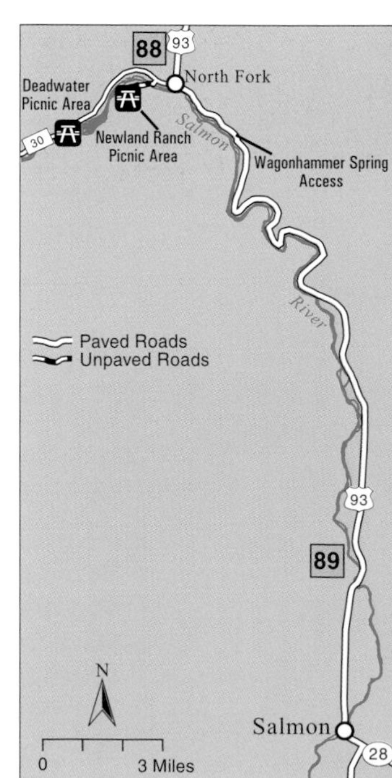

SITE NOTES: For river access, put in at North Fork and take out at Deadwater Picnic Area where there is an accessible ramp. North Fork Rd. (Forest Road 30) continues along the river and dead-ends at Corn Creek. Winter road maintenance is unpredictable. Maps and bird checklists are available at North Fork and Salmon.

CONTACT INFORMATION: USFS (208/865-2700), PVT

SIZE: 3.5 miles of river at Deadwater Slough, 46.4 river road miles along North Fork to Corn Creek Road

CLOSEST TOWN: North Fork

 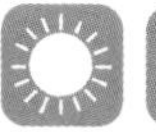  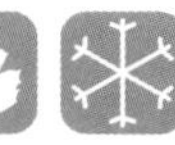

89 UPPER SALMON RIVER — SALMON TO NORTH FORK

Upper Salmon River © Leland Howard

DESCRIPTION: This 18-mile river stretch is a cottonwood riparian bottomland within a narrow valley flanked by the Beaverhead and Salmon River Mountains. About halfway downriver is Tower Creek Bottoms, a privately owned, 80-acre site that includes two ponds and a backwater slough with shrubby, as well as open, park-like areas.

VIEWING INFORMATION: View by canoe or from the main highway. Common spring and summer birds include the black-headed grosbeak, gray catbird, MacGillivray's warbler, yellow-headed blackbird, ruffed grouse, wood duck, Bullock's oriole, and Lewis's and pileated woodpeckers. There is a great blue heron rookery nearby. Along the river look for nest platforms used by osprey and Canada geese. Cliff swallows nest on river cliffs, and bobolinks nest in adjacent pastures. In winter, watch for bald eagles; year-round look for pronghorn, white-tailed and mule deer, and river otter.

SITE NOTES: See map on page 126. Rafters, kayakers, and canoers can use several small boat launches; inquire in Salmon at the BLM or USFS offices. Day hiking is available at Wagonhammer Springs. A bird checklist is available from the BLM in Salmon.

CONTACT INFORMATION: PVT, BLM (208/765-5400), USFS (208/865-2700)

SIZE: 18 miles of river

CLOSEST TOWN: Salmon

90 LEMHI RIVER — SALMON TO LEADORE

DESCRIPTION: This route travels through open sagebrush foothills and along large, shrubby, riparian zones of the Lemhi River. The route is interspersed with irrigated meadows and pastures.

VIEWING INFORMATION: Over 100 bird species are best viewed from May to July. Common species include great blue heron, great horned owl, American kestrel, red-tailed hawk, belted kingfisher, black-capped chickadee, warbling vireo, mountain bluebird, and song, vesper, Brewer's, and savannah sparrows. Less common are sandhill crane, short-eared owl, gray catbird, bobolink, lark bunting, Lewis's woodpecker, western wood-pewee, and common yellowthroat. Very few birds are present in fall and winter, but travelers at this time can look for rough-legged hawk, golden and bald eagles, and prairie falcon. Mule and white-tailed deer, pronghorn, and coyote can be seen year-round.

SITE NOTES: There is a small BLM campground five miles south of Lemhi on Idaho 28. Salmon has full facilities. A map and bird checklist are available at the USFS office in Salmon and Leadore.

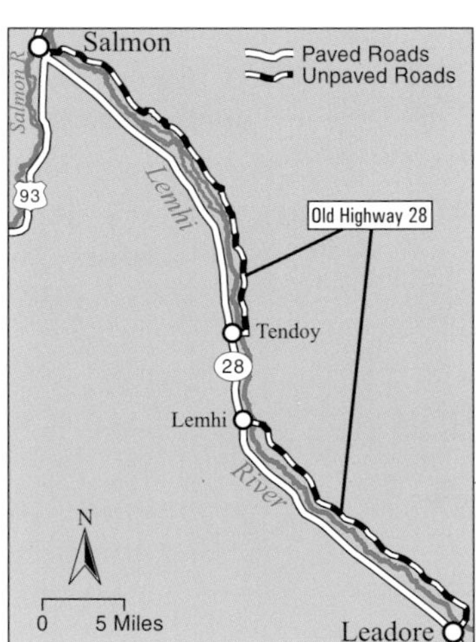

CONTACT INFORMATION: BLM (208/756-5400), PVT

SIZE: 45 miles of river

CLOSEST TOWN: Salmon

91 MORGAN CREEK

DESCRIPTION: Morgan Creek is an excellent place to view a variety of songbirds due to the diversity of habitats including shrub steppe, riparian areas, and timbered uplands.

Yellow-breasted chat © Colleen Sweeney

VIEWING INFORMATION: Common riparian birds include yellow and MacGillivray's warblers, warbling vireo, veery, lazuli bunting, willow flycatcher, song sparrow, and Brewer's and red-winged blackbirds. Major sagebrush species are Brewer's and vesper sparrows, sage thrasher, and rock wren. In timbered areas the hermit thrush, yellow-rumped warbler, pine siskin, dark-eyed junco, ruby-crowned kinglet, and Clark's nutcracker are common. Uncommon birds include Hammond's flycatcher, yellow-breasted chat, black-headed grosbeak, white-crowned and fox sparrows, gray catbird, Bullock's oriole, and pileated woodpecker. Look for bighorn sheep, elk, pronghorn, and mule deer in the hills from November to May.

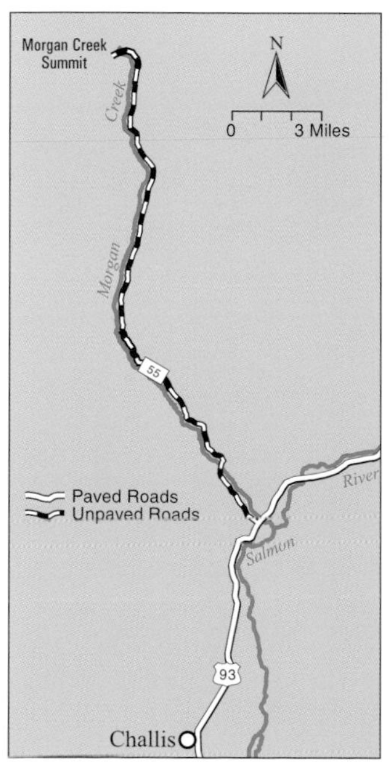

SITE NOTES: Five miles up Forest Road 55 is a BLM campground. Morgan Creek Summit is 19.4 miles from Hwy 93. More adventurous travelers may continue 44.8 miles down Panther Creek to the main Salmon River downstream of Shoup, traveling through the heart of the Salmon-Challis National Forest. Forest maps and a bird checklist are available from the USFS in Challis.

CONTACT INFORMATION: BLM (208/756-5400), USFS (208/879-4100), PVT

SIZE: 19 miles of creek

CLOSEST TOWN: Challis

92 SAWTOOTH FISH HATCHERY/INDIAN RIFFLES

DESCRIPTION: The Sawtooth Fish Hatchery features an information center with excellent displays on the life histories of anadromous fish, as well as views into the hatchery operations.

VIEWING INFORMATION: Visitors can see adult steelhead trout from March to May and the different life stages of chinook salmon year-round. The goal of the hatchery is to restore spring chinook salmon and steelhead trout to upper Salmon River tributaries. The Sawtooth Hatchery produces 2.4 million chinook salmon eggs each year. Chinook may grow to nearly 4 feet in length and weigh 50 pounds. In surrounding fields look for elk and deer in spring and winter. If you are visiting the area between March 15 and May 1 or late July to October 1, visit Indian Riffles to view migrating and spawning steelhead (spring) and chinook salmon (fall) in a natural stream setting. Also, look for common mergansers and great blue herons, often seen feeding on young fish.

SITE NOTES: Guided tours are conducted daily from Memorial Day through Labor Day.

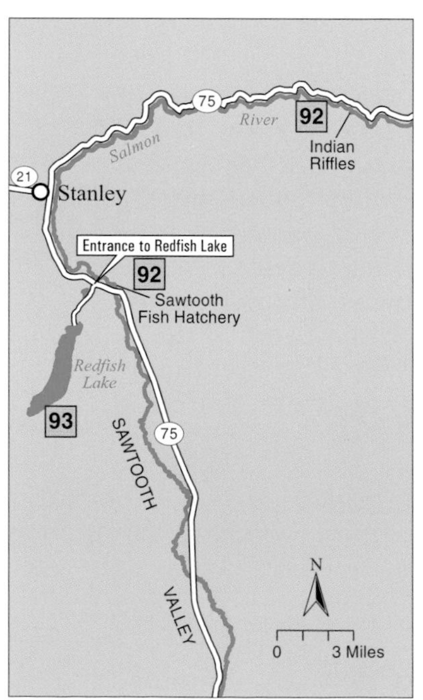

CONTACT INFORMATION: USFWS, managed by IDFG (208/774-3684)

SIZE: 100 acres

CLOSEST TOWN: Stanley

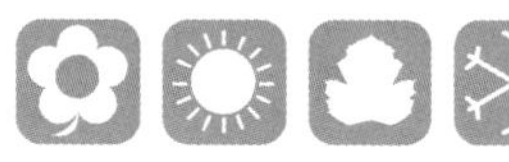

93 REDFISH LAKE/SAWTOOTH VALLEY

Red squirrel © Vitit Kantabutra

DESCRIPTION: This highly scenic valley is composed largely of sagebrush flats and grassy meadows bordered by lodgepole pine and aspen forests. Willows border the Salmon River and its tributaries, including Redfish Lake Creek. Redfish Lake is bordered by the rugged Sawtooth Mountains upstream and rimmed with coniferous forest on the remainder.

VIEWING INFORMATION: Leading from the Redfish Lake Visitor Center, the National Recreation Trail boardwalk traverses beaver habitat and offers Kokanee viewing over Fishhook Creek in early fall. Birding is good on the lake and at the mouth of Redfish Lake Creek, where forest trails lead to high mountain lakes in the Sawtooth Wilderness. Throughout forested areas the ruby-crowned kinglet, hermit thrush, Cassin's finch, yellow-rumped warbler, and woodpeckers are common. In willows along the lake, look for white-crowned, Lincoln's, and song sparrows and Townsend's, Wilson's, and yellow warblers. During spring and fall migration, check the lake for numerous waterfowl species and an occasional common loon. Frequently seen mammals are the yellow pine chipmunk, golden-mantled ground squirrel, red squirrel, coyote, and mule deer. Early summer wildflowers abound in the meadows. In winter observe bald eagles and notice snow tracks of red fox and wolverine around the lake. Another great viewing area is the Stanley Creek Wildlife Interpretive Area, a 40-acre wetland complex created by the confluence of Valley Creek, Stanley Creek, and Stanley Lake Creek.

SITE NOTES: See map on page 130. The Redfish Lake Visitor Center, open from mid-June to Labor Day, has maps, bird checklists, wildlife displays, interpretive programs, and hikes. The road to the lake is not plowed in winter, but used for cross-country skiing and snowmobiling.

CONTACT INFORMATION: USFS (Redfish Lake Visitor Center, summer: 208/774-3376; Stanley Ranger Station: 208/774-3000; Sawtooth National Recreation Area Headquarters: 208/727-5013)

SIZE: 1,600-acre lake **CLOSEST TOWN:** Stanley

94 EAST FORK SALMON RIVER CANYON

DESCRIPTION: The East Fork Salmon River and some of its feeder streams pass through both low and high elevational habitats. At 5,400 feet, sagebrush, cottonwood, riparian vegetation, and agricultural lands dominate the lower end of the river canyon. Big Boulder Creek Road traverses Douglas fir forest, sagebrush and willow/aspen riparian vegetation, climbing to subalpine forests of subalpine fir and whitebark pine bordering the White Cloud Peaks.

VIEWING INFORMATION: In the lower, open areas view chukar, red-tailed hawk, northern harrier, and occasionally, prairie falcon, pronghorn, and mule deer. Road Creek and Spar Canyon are good places to view the Challis wild horse herd. As you climb into alpine habitats, look for elk, bighorn sheep, golden eagle, and black rosy-finch. In most winters only the East Fork Road is open to travel, where visitors can see bighorn sheep, pronghorn and mule deer.

SITE NOTES: Jim Creek Road is rough and narrow and recommended for high-clearance 4-wheel drive vehicles only. A trail into the White Cloud Peaks starts from Jim Creek, or follow the road 5 miles to the top of Railroad Ridge. Sawtooth and Challis National Forest maps are available in Stanley or Challis. A bird checklist is available from the USFS office in Challis.

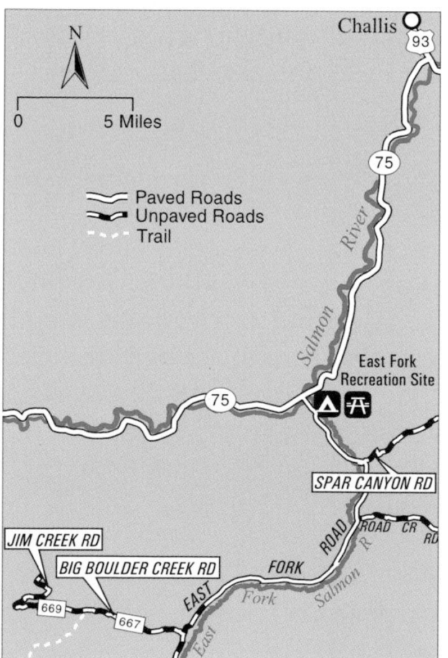

CONTACT INFORMATION: BLM (208/879-6200), USFS (208/774-3681 or 208/726-7672)

SIZE: 30-mile one-way drive

CLOSEST TOWN: Challis

95 MACKAY RESERVOIR/CHILLY SLOUGH

Chilly Slough © George Wuerthner

DESCRIPTION: Mackay Reservoir is set in sagebrush grassland habitat. The very upper end of the shoreline has mudflats even when the reservoir is full. Private lands border the mudflats, so the best view is from a boat or from the bluffs between U.S. 93 and the reservoir. Chilly Slough is a palustrine emergent wetland in the Big Lost River Valley with the 12,662-foot Mt. Borah towering to the east. From the parking area, visitors can walk along the marsh's edge.

VIEWING INFORMATION: Exposed mudflats at the reservoir in spring and fall attract numerous shorebirds and waterfowl, including cinnamon and green-winged teals, northern shoveler, pintail, and scaup. From spring through fall, Chilly Slough is rich with birds, including the birds listed above along with willet, sandhill crane, sora, marsh wren, savannah sparrow, red-tailed hawk, golden eagle, and northern harrier. Tundra swans are sometimes present in spring and fall. Several hundred pronghorn and mule deer winter in the sagebrush habitat east of U.S. 93 between Mackay Reservoir and Chilly Slough. Trout fishing is popular at Mackay Reservoir, where there are also kokanee. Chilly Slough supports spawning rainbow and brook trout. If you are heading to Challis between December and March, pull off the highway at Willow Creek Summit. Wintering elk can occasionally be seen feeding on curleaf mountain mahogany shrubs and bluebunch wheatgrass.

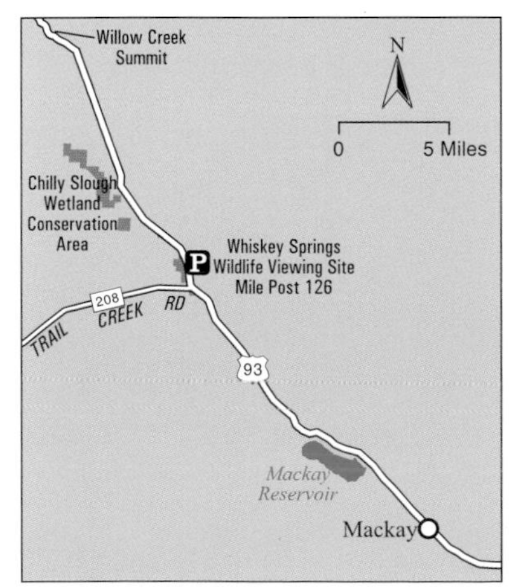

SITE NOTES: A bird checklist is available from the BLM or USFS offices in Salmon. Facilities listed are at Mackay Reservoir.

CONTACT INFORMATION: BLM (208/879-6200), IDFG (208/525-7290)

SIZE: 1,300-acre reservoir, 2041-acre Chilly Slough

CLOSEST TOWN: Mackay

96 TRAIL CREEK/CORRAL CREEK

Yellow-bellied marmot © Gary Kramer

DESCRIPTION: These mountain creek corridors, set in the upper reaches of a glacially carved valley, are rich in wildlife due to their habitat diversity. Riparian corridors are lined with aspen, alder, mature cottonwood, and willows. Nearby forest stands are a mix of Douglas fir and, at higher elevations, subalpine fir, limber pine, and whitebark pine. Talus slopes, cliffs, sagebrush, and avalanche chutes add to the diversity.

VIEWING INFORMATION: Common wildlife include the red-tailed hawk, northern harrier, blue grouse, red-naped sapsucker, American dipper, belted kingfisher, great blue heron, cinnamon teal and other ducks, red squirrel, Columbian ground squirrel, yellow-bellied marmot, elk, mule deer, and moose. Look for active beaver dams and rectangular holes made by pileated woodpeckers in large Douglas fir and cottonwood trees. Although quite rare, mountain goats have been seen in the rock cliffs of upper Trail Creek. Elk are most visible in winter when access is via cross-country skiing on Trail and Corral Creek Roads. There is a bluebird nest box trail along Corral Creek. Visit the Sawtooth National Recreation Area's Headquarters and Visitor Center for excellent wildlife displays, slide shows, literature, and checklists.

SITE NOTES: Viewing is from roads and short hikes off the roads. You can park at two overlooks along Trail Creek Road and at the Pioneer Cabin Trailhead; several loop trails from six to 20 miles depart from the trailhead. Pick up a bird checklist at the USFS Ketchum Ranger District office. Boundary Picnic Area with restrooms is about four miles past the Ketchum stoplight.

CONTACT INFORMATION: USFS (208/622-5371)

SIZE: 17 miles of road

CLOSEST TOWN: Sun Valley

   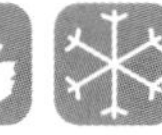

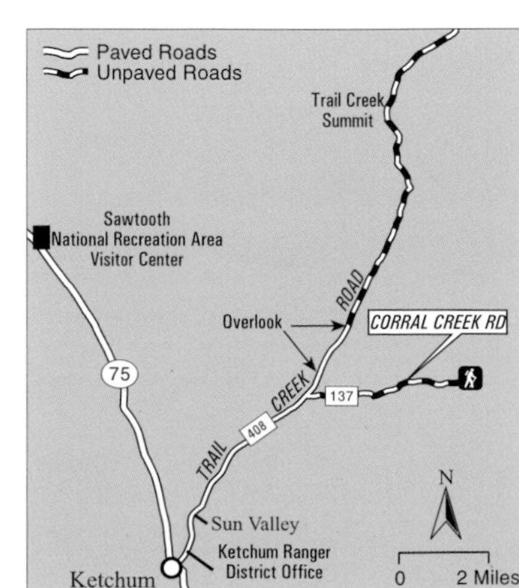

97 CAMAS PRAIRIE CENTENNIAL MARSH

DESCRIPTION: In spring, most of this 10,000-acre wet meadow is covered with shallow water, which starts to dry up in early July. Camas blooms in May cover the prairie with a purple blanket. Though a long history of farming has drastically altered the prairie from its natural state, the marsh is a wetland acquisition and restoration project supported by Ducks Unlimited, The Nature Conservancy, and the IDFG.

Camas in bloom at the Marsh © Craig Groves

VIEWING INFORMATION: On spring mornings the marsh is filled with thousands of shorebirds, wading birds, and waterfowl, including Wilson's phalarope, willet, Wilson's snipe, killdeer, sandhill crane, long-billed curlew, snow and Canada geese, canvasback, gadwall, and cinnamon, blue, and green-winged teals. Many of these species nest at the marsh. Raptors frequent the area including golden eagle, northern harrier, and red-tailed, rough-legged, and Swainson's hawks. The prairie is used as spring to fall range by mule deer and pronghorn. Elk winter on the prairie fringes. Introduced in 1986, several moose appear to be thriving. Coyote, red fox, badger, striped skunk, many small rodents, reptiles, and amphibians are found throughout the area. The best viewing is from spring to early summer. For additional viewing, Mormon Reservoir, five miles south of Fairfield, is home to a large ring-billed gull colony.

SITE NOTES: Drive, walk, or mountain bike the five miles of gravel roads.

CONTACT INFORMATION: IDFG (208/324-4359)

SIZE: 3,046 acres **CLOSEST TOWN:** Fairfield

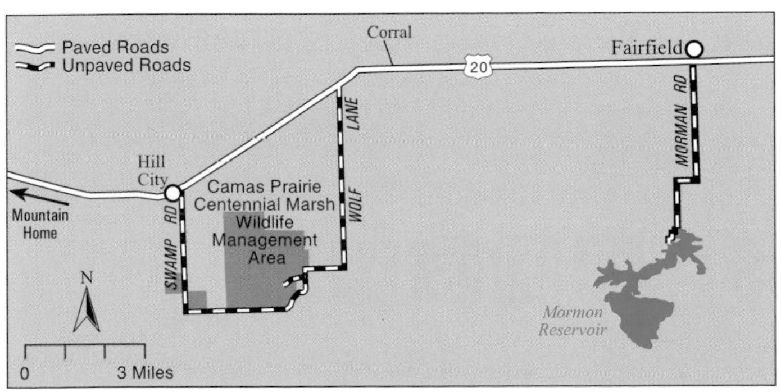

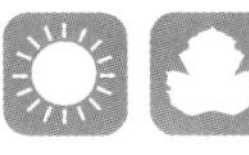

98 SILVER CREEK PRESERVE

Porcupine © Leland Howard

DESCRIPTION: This beautiful, meandering, spring-fed creek remains open all year and attracts an abundance of wildlife. Preserve land includes five miles of Silver Creek, its tributaries, and surrounding sagebrush desert. The Picabo Hills border the southern edge. This site is world renowned for its fly fishing.

VIEWING INFORMATION: View many waterfowl and wading birds, including goldeneye, sandhill crane, American bittern, and long-billed curlew. In sagebrush habitat look for sage grouse, vesper and Brewer's sparrows, and loggerhead shrike. Several warblers can be seen in willows and aspens along the creeks, including orange-crowned, yellow, yellow-rumped, MacGillivray's, and Wilson's warblers, plus the yellow-breasted chat. Uncommon birds seen during migration include osprey, merlin, tundra swan, northern mockingbird, and Caspian tern. Mammal inhabitants include striped skunk, river otter, beaver, mule deer, coyote, and porcupine. Bobcat, cougar, and elk are sometimes viewed in fall and winter. Moose pass through in spring and fall. Hiking and canoeing are popular year-round, while cross-country skiing is a favorite winter activity.

SITE NOTES: See map on page 137. Visit the preserve headquarters to sign in and pick up a map.

CONTACT INFORMATION: The Nature Conservancy (208/788-2203)

SIZE: 883 acres

CLOSEST TOWN: Picabo

99 CAREY LAKE WILDLIFE MANAGEMENT AREA

DESCRIPTION: This shallow, marshy lake is surrounded by irrigated pasture, hay and grain fields, sagebrush, and lava rock outcrops. The primary viewing is by small boat and from two parking areas by using binoculars or spotting scope.

VIEWING INFORMATION: Tundra swan, snow goose, and many other waterfowl species are often seen. Look for nesting Canada geese atop artificial platforms. Sandhill crane, American bittern, Virginia rail, American avocet, black-necked stilt, semipalmated plover, willet, lesser and greater yellowlegs, and pied-billed grebe are also regularly seen. American white pelican, hooded merganser, black tern, and American pipit are uncommon. Fishing and waterfowl hunting are popular; only non-motorized boats are allowed on the lake.

SITE NOTES: The WMA is on the south side of Highway 20 and visible from several turnoffs.

CONTACT INFORMATION: IDFG (208/324-4359)

SIZE: 750 acres

CLOSEST TOWN: Carey

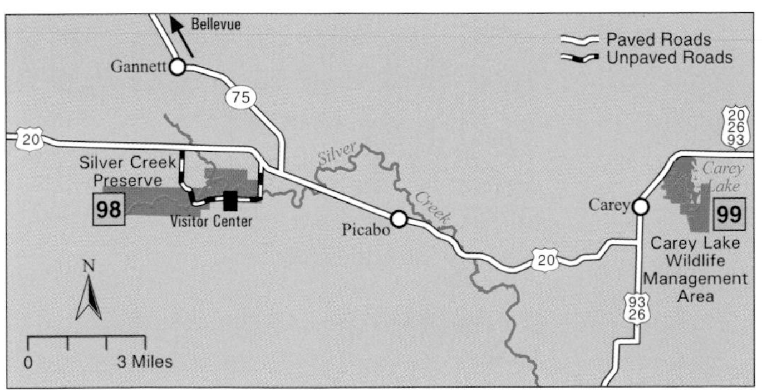

100 CRATERS OF THE MOON NATIONAL MONUMENT

Craters of the Moon National Monument
© David Clark

DESCRIPTION: This site's unusual "lunar" landscape is the result of the most recent lava flows on the Snake River Plain (only 2,000 years ago). Sporadic volcanic eruptions occurring over the last 15,000 years produced a mosaic of habitats, ranging from the barren lava flows of recent eruptions to older cinder cones with dense vegetation of sagebrush and grass. The dramatic basaltic formations provide a unique setting for wildlife-watching and photography.

VIEWING INFORMATION: In spring and summer, observe yellow-bellied marmot, pika, golden-mantled ground squirrel, red squirrel, blue and sage grouse, prairie falcon, and golden eagle. Look for nesting violet-green swallows, ravens, and great horned owls near the openings of lava tube caves. The mountain bluebird, state bird of Idaho, commonly nests in cavities of limber pines that grow on the lava flows and cinder cones. Other common birds include the black-capped and mountain chickadees, hairy woodpecker, Clark's nutcracker, common poorwill, and red-naped sapsucker. Reptiles warm themselves on the lava rock, so watch for racers, western rattlesnakes, gopher snakes, and short-horned and sagebrush lizards. June wildflower blooms can be spectacular. Fall visitors are likely to see mule deer and migratory songbirds. Though cross-country skiing is excellent, winter months may not be very rewarding for viewing wildlife.

0 20 Miles
Arco
Visitor Center
Carey
Craters of the Moon National Monument
Lake Walcott
Rupert
Burley

SITE NOTES: Drop in at the visitor center for maps and information about the wildlife, geology, and history of the area.

CONTACT INFORMATION: NPS (208/527-3257), BLM (208/732-7200)

SIZE: 754,862 acres

CLOSEST TOWN: Arco

WHERE TO FIND POPULAR WILDLIFE OF IDAHO

The index below lists some featured species in Idaho. The site numbers listed include areas where viewing opportunities are good. If the site is listed here, the species can be found there even if it's not listed in the text. This site list does not constitute the only places these species can be viewed. The numbers following each listing are site numbers. Check the Table of Contents to find the page numbers.

WATER BIRDS	SITE NUMBER
Canada goose	3, 27, 42, 58, 64, 84, 89
Common loon	8, 20, 35, 54, 65, 81, 93
Hooded merganser	11, 35, 75, 99
Snow goose	23, 39, 81, 83, 97, 99
Trumpeter swan	65, 71, 74, 77, 79, 81, 82
Black tern	74, 81, 99
Franklin's gull	75, 87
American white pelican	35, 48, 57, 58, 67, 81, 99

WADING BIRDS	SITE NUMBER
American bittern	23, 80, 83, 98, 99
Sandhill crane	35, 39, 72, 75, 78, 87, 97
Snowy egret	74, 81
White-faced ibis	38, 39, 67, 74, 75, 81, 83

UPLAND BIRDS	SITE NUMBER
Grey partridge	19, 31, 33, 85
Long-billed curlew	39, 52, 77, 80, 97, 99
Sage grouse	63, 79, 80, 85, 98, 100

SONGBIRDS	SITE NUMBER
Gray jay	6, 11, 17, 24, 36, 60
Lark bunting	47, 87, 90
Lewis's woodpecker	35, 47, 88, 90
Mountain bluebird	24, 36, 48, 62, 71, 73, 90
Steller's jay	6, 11, 17, 20, 24, 60
Willow flycatcher	47, 80, 91
Yellow-rumped warbler	24, 65, 85, 91, 93, 98

SHOREBIRDS	SITE NUMBER
Killdeer	12, 50, 52, 66, 97
Willet	66, 75, 80, 87, 95, 97, 99
Wilson's phalarope	37, 52, 75, 97
Yellowlegs	66, 99

SUPPORT IDAHO'S WATCHABLE WILDLIFE

Support Idaho's Nongame, Endangered, and Watchable Wildlife. Donations to the Idaho Nongame, Endangered, and Watchable Wildlife Program may be made to:

IDFG Nongame Trust Fund
P.O. Box 25, Boise, ID 83707

PLEASE HELP IMPROVE OUR NEXT GUIDE

The sponsors of this guide welcome comments concerning your experiences at viewing sites, adequacy of facilities, needs for interpretive information, accuracy of information, and usefulness of the guide. Please send your comments or recommendations to the Idaho Nongame, Endangered, and Watchable Wildlife Program, P.O. Box 25, Boise, ID 83707.

The Wildlife Conservation and Restoration Program (WCRP) is a 1-year appropriation from the Department of the Interior that offers financial and technical assistance for conservation programs that benefit each state's unique native fish and wildlife species and their habitats. A grant was received from WCRP to help fund the production of this Idaho Wildlife Viewing Guide. For more information on this and other wildlife grants in Idaho, contact Idaho Department of Fish and Game, 208/334-3700, P.O. Box 25, Boise, ID 83707.

ACKNOWLEDGMENTS

The Idaho Watchable Wildlife Committee would like to thank the following biologists, recreation specialists, managers, and others for their assistance with the production of this guide. This book could not be completed without your reviews of maps and site text, guidance through the process, and overall assistance. As we tried to name everyone, there are many more who assisted, and we thank you all. Names are listed in alphabetical order.

Bud Alford
Dennis Aslett
John Augsburger
Tom Bandalin
Fred Bear
Miles Benker
Steve Bouffard
Craig Brengle
Dan Brown
Dave Cannamella
Frances Cassirer
Joe Chapman
Dave Clark
Pat Cole
Dennis Coyle
Dan Davis
Mark Davidson
Betty Davenport
Mike Demick
Brad Dredge
Dennis Duehren
Gerry Deutscher
Terry Elms
Todd Fenzel
Mike Fisher
Mark Fleming
Nancy Freutel
Scott Gamo
Bill Gorgen
Terry Gregory
Jerry Gregson
Donna Griffin
KJ Hackworthy
Chuck Harris
Judi Hart
Curtis Hendricks
Tom Hess
Jena Hickey
Keith Hobbs
Rick Hobson
Geoff Hogander
Jody Holzworth
Wendy Hosman
Sandra Jacobson
Robin Jenkins
Juanita Jones
Trent Jones
Don Kemner
Bryan Kenworthy
Clair Kofoed
Stephanie Kukay
James Kumm
Bert Lewis
Michael Liner
Joseph Lowe
Tom Maeder
Jim Mallman
Michael Mancuso
Marie Marek
Allen May
Mike McDonald
Sam McNeil
Wayne Melquist
Robin Metz
Larry Mickelsen
Larry Mink
Carl Mitchell
Patti Murphy
Dave Musil
Blaine Newman
Kay Olpin
John O'Neill
Dick Orcutt
Anna Owsiak
Beth Paragamian
Dan Pennington
Pam Peterson
Von Pope
Kim Ragotzkie
Larry Ridenhour
Bryan Rowder
Vicky Runnoe
Dave Russel
Rex Sallabanks
Ted Scherff
Jerry Scholten
Warren Sedlacek
Sarah Sheldon
Tim Shelton
Dick Sjostrom
Pete Sozzi
Terry Thomas
Deb Tiller
Larry Townsend
Dave Trochlell
Paul Wackenhut
Jim White
Del Williams
Bill Whitaker
Scott Wright
Judi Zuckert
Kurt Zwolfer

IDAHO WATCHABLE WILDLIFE COMMITTEE MEMBERS

Jon Beals
Celeste Becia
Shelley Davis-Brunner
Alexis Collins
Steve Dunn
Bruce Haak
Mark Hilliard
Elaine Johnson
Jack Lavin
Meggan Laxalt Mackey
Wayne Melquist
Aimee Pope
Larry Ridenhour
R. L. Rowland
Kay Schiepan
Stephanie Singer
Jeff Stratten
Allan Thomas
Carl Wilgus